Collector's Guide to

Imperial Japanese Handguns

1893-1945

James D. Brown

Schiffer Military History
Atglen, PA

Book Design by Ian Robertson.

Library of Congress Control Number: 2007935204

Printed in China.
ISBN: 978-0-7643-2787-2

We are interested in hearing from authors with book ideas on related topics.

Published by Schiffer Publishing Ltd.
4880 Lower Valley Road
Atglen, PA 19310
Phone: (610) 593-1777
FAX: (610) 593-2002
E-mail: Info@schifferbooks.com.
Visit our web site at: www.schifferbooks.com
Please write for a free catalog.
This book may be purchased from the publisher.
Please include $3.95 postage.
Try your bookstore first.

In Europe, Schiffer books are distributed by:
Bushwood Books
6 Marksbury Avenue
Kew Gardens
Surrey TW9 4JF
England
Phone: 44 (0) 20 8392-8585
FAX: 44 (0) 20 8392-9876
E-mail: Info@bushwoodbooks.co.uk.
Free postage in the UK. Europe: air mail at cost.
Try your bookstore first.

Contents

Acknowledgments

This volume is a condensation of material presented in *Japanese Military Cartridge Handguns 1893-1945*. As such, it is ultimately based on the foundation laid by Harry L. Derby III in his original edition of *The Hand Cannons of Imperial Japan*, printed in 1981.

Although not the first serious student of Japanese military handgun development and history, Harry Derby has without doubt been the most significant pioneer in that work. He elevated the level of knowledge from a rather sparse summary of models and dates, laden with inaccuracies and downright myths, to a degree of sophistication and depth of understanding that has stood virtually unchallenged for more than twenty-five years. Other researchers, this author included, have built further on the foundation that Harry established as new specimens and records have been unearthed and analyzed, but one must search long and hard to find any of his conclusions that deserve *correction*, as opposed to refinement.

Harry has been, and continues to be, an inspiration to many collectors. He has examined—and in many cases owned—hundreds of Japanese military handguns and accessories, including specimens that were once thought to be merely oddities, but now are recognized as truly rare examples of the works of minor Japanese arms makers such as Kumazo Hino, Iwakichi Inagaki, and Bunji Hamada. He has also been either the discoverer of, or the first to unravel the significance of many of the creations of Imperial Japan's premier small arms designer and producer, Kijiro Nambu. His study of Japanese small arms has been remarkable, and he remains the foremost authority on that subject. His original work has itself become a cherished collectors' item.

Harry is an inspirational student of history, a charming and sometimes irascible companion, a doting grandfather, and a good friend. This publication would never have been produced if not for his influence.

***

Doss and Ruth White have published *BANZAI*, the Japanese military collectors' bulletin, for more than 20 years. Although not widely circulated, *BANZAI* provides a valuable forum for collectors to air their opinions and new findings on the subject matter, and fosters worldwide communication among students of Japanese weapons and history. Doss is himself an accomplished historian and collector, and during the preparation of *Japanese Military Cartridge Handguns 1893-1945* he asked if a condensed version for collectors could be compiled. He is thus the inspiration for this volume.

***

There have been a large number of individual collectors who have contributed, and continue to contribute, to the body of knowledge on Imperial Japanese handguns. One hundred and seventy-two of them are listed in the *Acknowledgments* section of *Japanese Military Cartridge Handguns 1893-1945*. Their contributions have been invaluable, and are deeply appreciated. The omission of a full list of their names here does not reflect any lack of gratitude, but instead is part of the overall effort to conserve space in this volume. Special thanks are due, however, to Teri Jane Bryant, Dale A. Crabtree, Dan Larkin, and Shin Nimura, who reviewed the draft of this volume, and provided many valuable comments and suggestions for its improvement. Annual production charts presented in Chapters VII and VIII are based on data provided by Dan Larkin.

Introduction

This volume has been prepared as an inexpensive guide to Japanese military handguns of the first half of the 20th century. It is intended primarily for the collector who, upon encountering a new specimen, wants information to identify, classify, and evaluate it in order to make a decision on its purchase. It will also be useful to dealers in establishing values, and to firearms owners who simply want to know where an individual pistol or its accessories fit in the overall picture of Japanese military collectibles. Foreign made handguns procured by the Japanese and used in military service are not covered in this work.

The subject of historical development of the different models and variants covered is not included in this work; readers desiring complete information in this area are referred to *Japanese Military Cartridge Handguns 1893-1945* by Derby and Brown, released by Schiffer Publishing, Ltd. in 2003. Japanese markings are covered in some detail, both to dispel the widespread lack of understanding of their meanings in the U.S., and because inspection marks define some rare variants, and can be used to determine whether components are original to a specimen or are replacements. The identification and naming of Japanese inspection marks, as presented in *Japanese Military Cartridge Handguns 1893-1945*, is vital to communication regarding these markings, and is incorporated in this text. Readers should note that in this context capitalized italics are used for *kanji* (Chinese characters adopted by the Japanese), while lower case italics are used for *kana* (Japanese characters representing phonetic syllables); this allows distinguishing between different characters with the same reading.

A brief word is in order on the origin of the name *Nambu*, which is commonly associated with Imperial Japanese handguns. Kijiro Nambu was born in 1869 to prominent Japanese parents. He chose a military career, and in 1897 was assigned to the Small Arms Section of the Tokyo Artillery Arsenal as a Captain. He was soon promoted to Major, and was assigned responsibility for developing Japan's first military semiautomatic pistol. His early work produced the "Grandpa," "Baby," and "Papa" Nambu pistols, all of which carry his name in *kanji* on the right side of their receivers. He eventually attained the rank of Major General, continuing to develop designs that produced the 1920 15-shot "Experimental" pistol, and eventually the Type 14. He retired in 1925, but continued to be active in arms production and development, designing and producing the Type 94 and, through his private Nambu Rifle Manufacturing Company in Kokubunji, Tokyo (later merged into the Chuo Kogyo Co., Ltd.), he also produced the Type 14, as well as a number of other military arms. He died in 1949 at the age of 80, but he remains the preeminent small arms designer of the Japanese Imperial Era, and his name is attached by some firearms enthusiasts to all Imperial Japanese handguns.

Organization of this volume mirrors that of *Japanese Military Cartridge Handguns 1893-1945*, with the exception that the chapters on foreign procurement and ammunition have been eliminated, and special naval pistols have been covered separately. Some models (the Hino, the Mark A Experimental, Hamada, Inagaki, North China Type 19, Sugiura, and Special Naval pistols) are given only very brief treatment, primarily because their scarcity significantly limits the number of readers who will be directly interested in them. Instead, emphasis is placed on the two most commonly encountered models, the Types 14 and 94, and secondarily on the Type 26 revolver and the "Grandpa," "Papa," and "Baby" Nambu pistols. In the Type 14 and Type 94 chapters, the numerous variants are discussed in detail.

Serial number and date ranges, as well as total production figures presented for variations are estimates based on observed specimens. Because of the gaps that exist between specimens that have been examined, it is likely that other examples will be found that fall slightly outside of the estimated ranges. Occasionally, specimens are encountered that are well outside of expectations; this is explained in the "out of sequence" and "off-date" sections of the Type 14 and Type 94 chapters. Collectors are urged to report all specimens, regardless of their apparent scarcity or uniqueness, to Mike and Dan Larkin, who have maintained a database on the subject for more than 25 years that forms the basis for much related research. Reporting of specimens does not constitute registration or imply ownership of the pistols reported. Contact Dan by e-mail at dlarkin@co.humboldt.ca.us, or by telephone at (707) 443-4223, and provide the pistol's model, serial number, and date; other pertinent information will then be requested as needed.

For those with questions or a need for clarification or additional information, an e-mail address has been established at nambukenjyu@hotmail.com. This mailbox is monitored regularly, and interested readers are encouraged to use it to contact the author.

Strategies for collecting Japanese military handguns can be as simple or as complex as the interest and budget of the collector allows. The rarer models—the 1902 "Grandpa" Nambu and the eight "minor" semiautomatics—are out of the reach of most collectors because of their scarcity and high cost. The "Papa" Nambu offers an array of ten recognized variations, although finding them all in fine condition is quite challenging. The "Baby" Nambu offers two primary variants, plus the rare "imperial gift" presentation pieces. The Type 26 revolver offers five variations.

The two more common models, the Types 14 and 94, offer much more collecting variety because of their greater numbers, and the use of era dates to signify their year and month of manufacture. Although some collectors are happy to have a single representative example of each type, those wishing for a greater challenge can find it quite easily. The Type 14 was produced by five different manufacturers (five basic variants), two of whom produced two different serial series (bringing the total to seven variants). Seeking a specimen from each manufacturer for each production year brings the total number of variants to 33, or 35 if you include both serial series for transitional years; only two collections are known to have achieved this objective. There are also variations based on manufacturing changes, and some collectors seek to "bracket" these changes as closely as possible with specimens produced just before and just after the change. There are prototypes, cutaways, "last-ditch" examples, and other specialized or unique pieces to add depth to a collection. The Type 94 had only one manufacturer and eleven production years, but to these 11 basic variants can be added marking and manufacturing changes that bring the total number of recognized variants to at least 20. For a truly challenging collection, one can seek to acquire a specimen from each manufacturer for every month of production: a total of 329 for the Type 14, and 111 for the Type 94 (there are some months during the production periods of both models in which no pistols are known to have been produced, for a variety of reasons). This has been attempted but not yet achieved, even though one major collection contains more than 500 examples of these two models.

One of the challenges of collecting Japanese military handguns is simply finding specimens for sale; one cannot simply call "Nambu Central" and put in an order for a TGE "Baby" or a *Taisho*-era Type 14. Individual Japanese pistols do turn up occasionally at gun stores and pawnshops, but larger regional gun and military shows generally present a better opportunity for finding interesting specimens. For those familiar with the internet, the GunBroker.com and AuctionArms.com websites frequently offer Japanese handguns for sale, but one must understand the risks inherent in bidding on a firearm that one has not personally examined—it may or may not be as described, subject both to the seller's integrity and to the level of their knowledge of Japanese weapons. Ask questions before you bid, and if possible secure a 3-day return option pending your examination. In addition to online auction sites, there are a number of dealers in collectible arms that include Japanese weapons in their electronic offerings, but most of these tend to be near the upper end of the price scale. Any internet purchase of a firearm, and any out-of-state purchase of a cartridge handgun not made prior to 1898, must be transferred through a Federal Firearms Licensee. All of the handguns covered in this volume qualify as "Curios and Relics" under Federal law.

It must be borne in mind that the entire universe of Japanese military cartridge handgun production from 1893 through 1945 encompasses fewer than 500,000 guns. In contrast, the U.S. Government procured more than 2.8 million .45 automatic pistols, 330,000 .45 caliber revolvers, and over 1 million .38 caliber revolvers in the same period. Military production of the P.08 Luger by Germany exceeded 2.5 million pistols through the end of World War II, to say nothing of the millions of Mausers, Walthers, Sauers, and foreign pistols produced under German occupation and issued to their troops. The comparatively modest prices of Japanese military pistols in relation to their American and European counterparts is not well correlated to their scarcity, and can only be explained by their lack of familiarity and appreciation among the larger firearms collecting community.

A statement on current valuation is presented near the end of each chapter covering the models included. However, one must remember that the wide array of variants involved makes it impossible to establish a general value that can be applied to all, or even most, pistols of a type. Some sellers offer relatively common pistols at elevated prices because of lack of familiarity and misperceptions of their rarity; conversely, truly rare specimens are sometimes sold for far less than their true worth because the seller is ignorant of their significance. Figures offered in this volume are intended to provide guidance, but are by no means absolute or infallible. When considering the purchase of one of the rarer pistols or variants, it is always advisable to solicit the opinions of more than one expert, bearing in mind that an evaluation or appraisal without firsthand examination is marginal at best.

Twentieth Century Japanese military handguns present an interesting window into the mechanical ingenuity and culture of the people who made and used them, and a historical perspective on the increasing strain placed on the Japanese arms industry during the course of the Second World War. They are fascinating to study, and can also be valuable investments.

Identification Key

Dichotomous Key to Imperial Japanese Handgun Identification

(Not including prototypes or foreign-procured weapons)

1. Handgun is self-loading; breech closure is by slide or bolt moving in line with bore or by reciprocating barrel....2
1. Handgun is not self-loading; breech closure is hinged....14
    2. Barrel fully exposed, not covered by a slide or jacket....3
    2. Barrel fully or mostly covered by a slide or jacket....8
        3. Trigger guard is an integral part of the receiver.... **North China Type 19** (Chapter 9)
        3. Trigger guard is a separate assembly fitted into the receiver....4
            4. Pistol has grip safety located immediately below bottom of trigger guard....5
            4. Pistol has no grip safety....7
                5. Pistol overall length approximately 6¾ inches, rear sight fixed.... **"Baby" Nambu** (Chapter 5)
                5. Pistol overall length approximately 9 inches, rear sight tangent adjustable....6
                    6. Trigger guard inside diameter approximately 1 inch.... **"Grandpa" Nambu** (Chapter 3)
                    6. Trigger guard inside diameter approximately 1¼ inch.... **"Papa" Nambu** (Chapter 4)
                7. Top of barrel extension and bolt rounded, rear sight fixed.... **Type 14** (Chapter 7)
                7. Top of barrel extension and bolt flat, rear sight tangent adjustable.... **Mark A Experimental** (Chapter 6)
            8. Barrel covering is a non-movable jacket integral with receiver.... **Hino** (Chapter 2)
            8. Barrel covering is a moveable slide....9
                9. Rear of slide passes through raised receiver bridge bearing rear sight.... **Type 94** (Chapter 8)
                9. Rear of slide does not pass through a raised receiver bridge....10
                    10. Muzzle protrudes significantly (approximately ½ inch) beyond front of slide.... **Inagaki** (Chapter 10)
                    10. Muzzle approximately flush with front of slide....11
                        11. Rear of slide with six wide, widely-spaced, square-bottomed gripping grooves....12
                        11. Rear of slide with fifteen or more narrow, v-shaped gripping grooves....13
                            12. Top rear of slide has large, semicircular weight-reduction cut on each side.... **Type 2 Hamada** (Chapter 9)
                            12. Top rear of slide has no weight reduction cuts.... **7.65 mm Hamada** (Chapter 9)
                            13. Pistol overall length approximately 5½ inches.... **6.35 mm Sugiura** (Chapter 12)
                            13. Pistol overall length approximately 7 inches.... **7.65 mm Sugiura** (Chapter XII)
        14. Handgun is a revolver.... **Type 26** (Chapter 1)
        14. Handgun is not a revolver....15
            15. Bore diameter greater than 1¼ inch.... **Type 10 Signal Pistol** (Chapter 14)
            15. Bore diameter less than 1¼ inch....16
            16. Bore diameter greater than 1 inch....17
            16. Bore diameter less than 1 inch....19
                17. Two-barrel pistol with external hammers.... **Kayaba Double Barrel Signal Pistol** (Chapter 14)
                17. Single or multiple-barrel pistol without hammer....18
                    18. Single-barrel pistol.... **KFC Type 97 Signal Pistol** (Chapter 14)
                    18. Two- or three-barrel pistol.... **Kayaba Type 90 Signal Pistol** (Chapter 14)
                19. Single-barrel pistol.... **"Type 5" Special Naval Pistol** (Chapter 13)
                19. Double-barrel pistol.... **Type 4 Special Naval Pistol** (Chapter 13)

I

The Type 26

The Type 26 was the first cartridge handgun of native design adopted by the Japanese military; it was also the only revolver produced by Japan prior to the end of World War II. Its designation is derived from the date of its adoption, the 26th year of the *Meiji* Era (1893). The Type 26 is a double-action-only design based primarily on the Austrian Rast-Gasser. It is chambered for the relatively low-powered 9x23 mm Japanese revolver cartridge, which was not used in any other firearm.

Total production of the Type 26 reached slightly less than 60,000 guns. These are classified into four primary production variants, plus a fifth variant that consists of revolvers from the first three variants that were returned to the arsenal for rebuilding that generally included replacement of grip panels, upgrading exterior markings on early production guns, and refinishing. Manufacture of the Type 26 was conducted at the Tokyo Artillery Arsenal between 1893 and about 1925, with a small late production run at some point between 1926 and 1935 (the date of this final run is not known). Arsenal rebuilding of the Type 26 was also carried out at Tokyo, although there is evidence that some individual revolvers were repaired by other arsenals after 1935.

Early (above) and late production examples of the Type 26.

The Type 26 has never been widely popular among collectors. It is, nonetheless, a significant milestone in the development of Japan's arms industry. Because of a long service history, much of it in second-class status, most examples show extensive exterior wear. For this reason, however, any specimen in fine original condition should be considered a collector's prize, especially if it is an example of the rare first, second, or fourth variants.

Identification

The Type 26 is a 9 mm six-shot revolver with a top-break loading design, automatic extraction, a two-course cylinder, a spurless hammer with fixed firing pin, a rounded butt cap with lanyard ring, and either checkered or horizontally grooved wooden grip panels. The cylinder's rear course is 38 mm in diameter with locking notches; the forward course is 36 mm in diameter and is fluted. The barrel extension forward of the cylinder latch has a raised channel 32 mm long that is machined to form the rear sight; the front sight is semicircular, and is pinned to a raised base at the front of the barrel. The revolver has an overall length of 231 mm (9.09"), a barrel length of 121 mm (4.76"), and an unloaded weight of 2 lbs. Its left sideplate is hinged at the rear, so that when unlocked by disengaging and lowering the rear of the trigger guard, it can be swung outward to expose the lockwork. The rear of the trigger guard is knurled to facilitate this action.

Markings

With the exception of unmodified first variation specimens, the Type 26 is stamped on the right side of the receiver below the hammer with the arsenal symbol and type *kanji* (reading, from left to right, "Two Ten Six [26] Year Type"). The serial number is stamped below the type *kanji* on all but first and second variation specimens. One or more inspection marks will also be found stamped on the butt cap. A typical example of the right side markings is:

ஃ	Tokyo Arsenal symbol
二十六年式	Type designation *kanji*
11301	Serial number

As noted above, unmodified first variation specimens will have no right side markings, while unmodified second variation specimens will carry the arsenal symbol and type *kanji*, but no external serial number. First and second variation guns that have been arsenal rebuilt will have had full right-side markings applied at the time of rebuilding, making positive variant identification extremely difficult. Early third variation guns (through approximately serial #10,000) have very lightly stamped type *kanji*; on rebuilt specimens, these markings have usually been re-stamped, and evidence of this modification can often be detected by careful examination with a 10x lens.

Internal markings of the Type 26 involve assembly and subassembly numbers on most parts. The method of assigning these numbers was changed more than once during the course of production. On the first 10,000 guns, the assembly number is the same as the serial number. When production reached five-digit serial numbers, a decision was made to limit the assembly number to three digits, accompanied by a series prefix in the form of a *kana* character. The primary assembly number is stamped on the left side of the grip frame under the panel, with the series prefix generally above and/or to the left of the assembly number itself. On serial #11301, for example, the assembly number and its prefix are marked:

イ
971

The assembly number is stamped on most internal parts; separate sub-assembly numbers (unrelated to the assembly number) are stamped on the hammer, cylinder, and barrel hinge of most specimens. (Only the hammer always carries all of these numbers; it is thus the best indicator of whether other parts are matching.) Assembly number prefixes were assigned to blocks of 1,000 receivers following the order of the poem *Iroha*, with the "original" (10,000 serial block) carrying no prefix. Fabrication of receivers and parts evidently outpaced revolver assembly, producing irregularities in the relationship between assembly and serial numbers. By the 35,000 serial range, parts fabrication had evidently been terminated, and all assembly was being done from parts in storage, as the assembly prefix sequence breaks down completely at this point. On fourth variation guns, assembly numbers are the last two digits of the serial number, and no prefixes or sub-assembly numbers are used. The receivers for these revolvers were clearly fabricated much later than those for the standard production run.

Variations

1. Early production – no external markings: Some of the first revolvers produced carried no external markings; all reported examples are serialized below 300. Two later specimens, serial numbers 8258 and 8259, also lack external markings. Because many of these guns saw extensive service and were later rebuilt, external arsenal, type, and serial markings have often been added, obscuring the first variation identity of these specimens. Original revolvers of this variant have charcoal blueing and heat-blued hammers.

2. Early production – external arsenal and type markings only: Mixed with the first and third variations, some reported specimens have external arsenal and type markings, but no external serial numbers. Most reported specimens fall below serial #900, but three higher specimens have been reported (serial numbers 4925, 5262, and 9366). As with first variation guns, many second variation revolvers were rebuilt, adding external serial numbers and obscuring their original identity. Original finish characteristics are identical to the first variation.

3. Standard production: The great majority of all Type 26s fall into this category, which includes most revolvers from serial #900 through 58,900. During the standard production period a number of minor manufacturing changes occurred, including the depth of markings, the length of the trigger guard, locations of inspection markings, and the phased-in substitution of grooved rather than checkered grip panels after about serial #54,000. However, the lack of precise definition of these changes, combined with relatively low collector interest, has precluded identifying these as sub-variants.

4. Limited modified final production: After regular production of the Type 26 had ended, a final limited production run of approximately 300 guns was made, probably in coordination with the recall and rebuilding of worn and damaged revolvers from earlier production. The range of reported serial numbers for this variant is 58903-59227. All observed specimens have rust blued finishes and grooved grip panels and, as noted above, their assembly numbers are the last two serial digits, with no prefix. Two different types of knurling may be found on the trigger guards of these pistols: the standard checkered type, and a simpler serrated type.

5. Arsenal rebuilds: This variant consists of specimens from the first three variations that were returned to the arsenal for major overhaul and refurbishing. Worn or damaged parts have been replaced—often without regard to earlier numbering—external markings have been brought up to period standards, the exterior has been refinished with a rust blue, and in many cases original grip panels have been replaced with the later grooved design. The number of examples of this variant can only be guessed from its relative abundance among earlier specimens, but it is estimated to be between 2,500 and 4,000.

Values

Values of Type 26s are highly variable, depending upon condition and production variant. Currently, a run-of-the-mill specimen with most of its original finish will bring $250 to $350, while a rare variant in fine original condition may command a price of $1,200 or more. There is little market for heavily worn specimens, even as "parts guns."

Accessories

The Type 26 was issued with a leather clamshell holster with shoulder strap, a braided cotton lanyard, a cleaning rod, and a box of 50 cartridges. Early holsters were black, and were accompanied by dark blue lanyards; general production holsters are brown, and are found with tan or light green lanyards. A very late holster variant was made of canvas with leather fittings. Both the early and late holsters are very rare, although the mid-production type is not uncommon. A reproduction leather holster and strap has recently been imported; it can be distinguished from the original by the latchplate rivet pattern (see Chapter V).

Original cleaning rods are steel or nickeled steel, 177 mm long, with a closed offset oval loop handle at one end and a patch slot at the other. They are quite rare. Other types of rods, including those intended for use with other weapons, are often encountered with the Type 26.

Ammunition for the Type 26 was packaged in boxes made of brown cardboard, with the weapon identification printed on the top, as shown below. The first line is arranged in a circle around the arsenal symbol, while the second line is horizontal. Full boxes of original ammunition are rare, and even single cartridges are scarce.

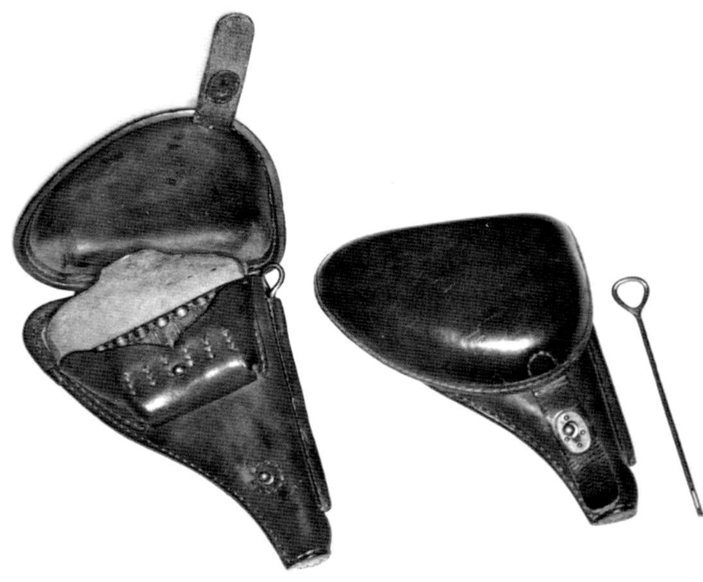

Type 26 holsters, open and closed, and cleaning rod. *Courtesy Harry L. Derby III.*

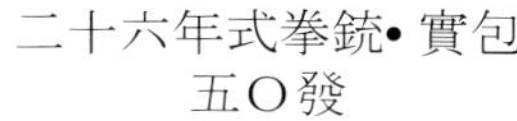

二十六年式拳銃• 實包
五O發

II

The Hino

The Hino, or Hino-Komuro, is an unusual but interesting handgun design. The pistol was developed by Kumazo Hino; production was supported by Tomojiro Komuro, who provided the manufacturing facility. The Hino was never adopted for military use, but individual guns were privately procured and carried by some Japanese officers, and there is evidence that Japanese Ordnance toyed with the idea of modernizing a small stock of them for limited military use in the years prior to World War II.

The Hino is an example of the "blow-forward" mechanical design, shared only with the later Austrian Schwarzlose. Mechanically, it is quite simple, but in operation it requires more effort by the user to initiate a first shot than is normal for a semiautomatic handgun, possibly explaining its sparse production and limited sales. It might be described as an elegant but awkward pistol.

Identification

All Hinos were basically hand-made, and differ from one another in minor details. The barrel, which is 194 mm (7.64") long in the 7.65 mm model and 217 mm (8.54") long in the 8 mm model, is largely contained within the receiver, with a portion of the muzzle protruding from the front. The design lacks a trigger guard, but includes a grip safety located just below the trigger on the forward grip strap. A button-type magazine catch is located in the upper section of the left grip panel just behind the trigger. The barrel protrudes forward from its housing, and is serrated on the sides to facilitate cocking, which involves pulling it forward 38 mm (1.5") to latch it in the open position. Grip panels are of finely checkered and bordered walnut. A lanyard loop is provided at the lower end of the rear grip strap.

Markings are limited to the serial number stamped on most parts and the following inscription on the rear grip strap:

小 [encircled]
特許
7165
乙
31
圧

The encircled *kanji* character 小 (*KO*) was evidently a trademark derived from the first character in Komuro's name (小室). The *kanji* 特許 is translated "patent," and is followed by the pat-

Hino pistol serial number 184. *Steve Fox Collection.*

ent number; 乙 means "series," and is followed by the serial number (31 in this example); and the character 圧 means "pressure," and is evidently an indication that the pistol was test fired with a proof load.

Although the inventor apparently intended to offer the pistol in a fairly wide array of chamberings, all but two known examples fire the 7.65 mm Browning (.32 ACP) cartridge. The exceptions, one in a private U.S. collection and the other housed at Scotland Yard, are chambered for the 8 mm Nambu cartridge. The 7.65 mm Hinō varies from 237 to 256 mm (9.3" to 10.1") in length and weighs 1 lb 8 oz; the 8 mm model is 265 mm (10.4") in length, and weighs 2 lbs. Both models have a magazine capacity of eight cartridges.

Thirty-three specimens of the Hino are known from a total production of approximately 450 pistols. Ten of these, unfortunately, are scheduled to be destroyed by the Japanese government because they are in technical violation of that country's firearms registration law. Nine other specimens are in Japanese museums or police reference collections. For all practical purposes, this pistol is unavailable to collectors unless a new specimen is discovered, or a current owner disposes of his collection. Any attempt at establishing a value is thus speculative; prices will be determined by the seller's advertising skill, and the bidding audience available at the time of the sale. Known sale prices in recent years range from $2,000 for an incomplete but restorable specimen in fair condition to $12,500 for a very good 7.65 mm example.

III

The 1902 Nambu Type "Grandpa"

The first commercially produced Japanese semiautomatic pistol was the 8 mm Nambu Type, developed by Major (later Major General) Kijiro Nambu, and introduced in 1902, *Meiji* 35. However, because it was never officially adopted by the Japanese military, it was named "Nambu Type" for its designer, rather than being given an era year designation. To collectors, it is commonly known as the "Grandpa" Nambu. The development of the 1902 Nambu Type included the purchase, examination, and analysis of all of the major semiautomatic designs of the period; elements of some of these designs can be seen in the "Grandpa," but there are also a number of features that are unique. The 1902 Nambu is thus a blend of contemporary ideas from other designers and those that are original Nambu.

Although the "Grandpa" was manufactured by the Tokyo Artillery Arsenal, it was available for private purchase both by Japanese officers and by private civilians. Because most "Grandpas" were privately owned, they were generally well cared for, and the majority of surviving specimens are in surprisingly good condition. Approximately 2,400 "Grandpas" were produced between 1903 and 1906. Of these, approximately 350 were sold to Thailand; efforts were also made to market the "Grandpa" in China, but there is no evidence that this led to any significant sales.

1904 "Grandpa" Nambu serial number 195. *Courtesy Harry L. Derby III.*

The "Grandpa" is a historically significant, finely crafted pistol. Exterior metal surfaces are rust blued, except for the trigger and magazine latch, which are heat-treated to a "straw" color. The bolt and the inner faces of the ejection port are unblued. The magazine body is nickel plated. "Grandpas" are highly prized collectors' items.

Identification

The "Grandpa" Nambu is an 8 mm semiautomatic pistol with an exposed barrel, an adjustable tangent rear sight, a single recoil spring located in a tunnel on the left side of the receiver, a 68 degree angled grip with fully checkered walnut panels, a grip safety located on the front strap, and a small (20 mm diameter) circular trigger guard. It is similar in size and appearance to the "Papa" Nambu (see Chapter 4) except for the smaller trigger guard and the magazine base, which is made of checkered oak. The pistol is 230 mm (9.06") long, and weighs 2 lbs. It has a magazine capacity of eight cartridges, which is retained in the pistol by a push-button latch located in the left grip panel behind the trigger. A fixed lanyard loop is located on the rear of the receiver just below the cocking knob. The rear grip strap is slotted to accept a shoulder stock.

Field Disassembly

Clear the pistol by removing the magazine to ensure that it is empty, pull the cocking knob approximately ½" to the rear (but do not fully cock the pistol), and inspect the chamber to make sure it is not loaded. Replace the magazine, and pull the trigger to make sure the pistol is uncocked, then remove the magazine.

Push in on the bolt lock, located on the rear of the cocking knob, and rotate it counter-clockwise ¼ turn, aligning its index mark with the mark at nine o'clock on the cocking knob. Withdraw the lock to the rear out of the cocking knob.

Press the muzzle against a firm surface, pushing the barrel extension to the rear approximately 3 mm. While maintaining rearward pressure on the barrel extension, push the magazine latch button in as far as it will go and slide the trigger guard downward into the safety well until it stops.

Withdraw the barrel extension assembly forward out of the receiver. Rotate the rear of the locking block downward and remove it, then withdraw the bolt and striker from the rear of the barrel extension and separate them.

Use the bolt lock as a tool to push the recoil spring guide to the rear far enough for the cocking knob to clear the lanyard loop, and unscrew the knob from the end of the guide; withdraw the spring and its guide forward out of the receiver. (In reassembling these parts, the lug on the front of the spring guide must be aligned with its receiver recess, and the cocking knob must be indexed with the mark on the rear of the guide.)

Remove the grip panel screws, and remove the grip panels by raising their lower edge and slipping them downward off of the receiver.

Markings

The right rear of the "Grandpa's" receiver carries the stamped *kanji* 式部南, reading from right to left, "Nambu Type," above the serial number. The top of the chamber carries the Tokyo Arsenal symbol ⛭. Small inspection marks may be stamped on the lower front grip strap, or inside of the grip safety well. Thai-purchased pistols will have a circular *Charka* (❁) crest stamped on either the front or rear strap.

Variations

Because the "Grandpa" was produced for only a relatively brief period, no major changes were made in its design during production. Serial #1, which could have been Kijiro Nambu's prototype of the design, differs from standard production "Grandpas" in minor ways, including the use of a coil rather than a leaf spring for the trigger, and the use of horn rather than wood for the magazine bases.

Several "transitional" pistols are known, including serial nos. 2052, 2054, 2091, 2151, 2156, 2185, and 2332. These pistols have one or more features of the later "Papa" design, including movable lanyard loops, aluminum magazine bases, and modified grip frames, trigger guards, barrel extensions, and bolts. Some of these transitional pistols also have additional mechanical modifications, such as relocation of the sear bar pin, and use of the "Papa" sear bar design.

Since most "Grandpas" were privately purchased they were generally well cared for, and often remain in very good to excellent condition even today. Typically, values for such pistols start at around $7,500, and rise significantly when accompanied by an original shoulder stock and accessories. Very early specimens, the rare transitional variants, and complete pistol/accessory sets in fine original condition may command prices of $15,000 or more.

Accessories

It is believed that all "Grandpas" were originally produced with individually fitted and serial numbered shoulder stocks made of cherry wood that also served as holsters. These stocks are found in two sizes, the principle difference being that the "large" stock is approximately 12 mm (0.5") greater in its top-to-bottom dimension than the "small" one. The shoulder stocks have a hinged butt that opens to provide access to the storage recesses for the pistol, spare magazine, and cleaning rod (Serial # 1 has no cleaning rod recess.). The forward end of the stock has a tubular metal extension that adds 80 mm (3.1") to the stock's length; a checkered steel button locks it in either the retracted or extended position. The right side of the stock is fitted with a metal harness plate with three loops for attaching a leather carrying harness.

Leather holsters were also made available for the "Grandpa," but they were apparently seldom used, and are very rare. They

Large (above) and small Nambu shoulder-stocks, extended, right side view. *Courtesy Harry L. Derby III.*

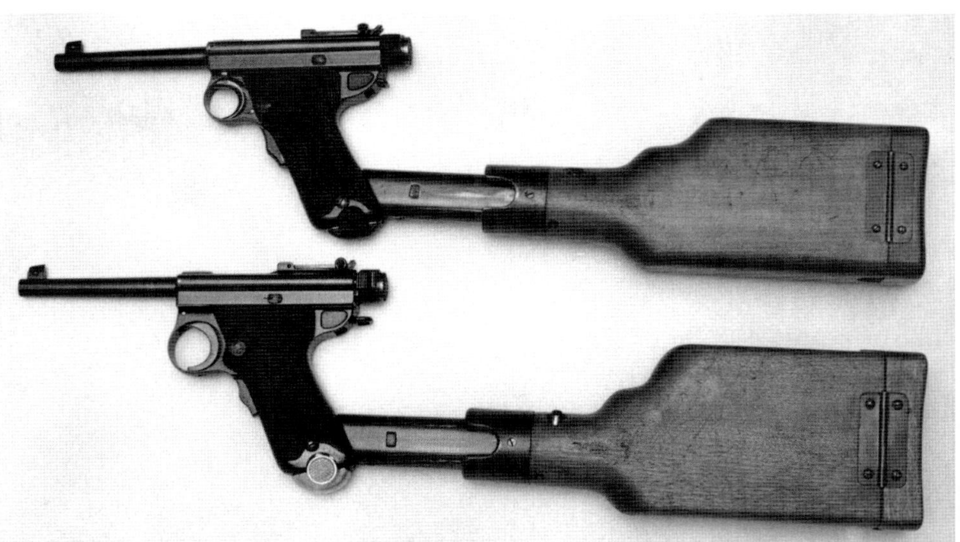

"Grandpa" (above) and "Papa" Nambu pistols fitted with shoulder-stocks, left side view. *Courtesy Harry L. Derby III.*

employ a hard clamshell closure design, and differ from the more common "Papa" holster in that they do not have a spare ammunition pouch located under the closure flap.

A cleaning rod of nickel plated steel was produced for the "Grandpa." It is "L" shaped, with the long segment being 145 mm in length, while the short "handle" segment is only 10 mm long. The end opposite the handle is flattened, and has a patch slot and a screwdriver tip.

Standard cotton lanyards were also provided for the "Grandpa." Original lanyards are tan in color, with leather slides and keepers.

Ammunition for the Nambu Type pistols was packed in 50-round brown cardboard boxes sealed with paper. The earliest known specimens are labeled for the "Army Type Handgun" (the "Papa"). Based on other cartridge box markings, it can be assumed that the earliest boxes would have been labeled for the "Nambu Type Handgun," but no surviving examples are known.

IV

The Modified 1902 Nambu Type "Papa"

By 1904, Kijiro Nambu had prepared revisions to his original 1902 design, apparently to eliminate shortcomings that had become evident through field use, and possibly also to simplify manufacture. The resulting "Modified Nambu Automatic Pistol Type A' went into production in about 1906, replacing the 1902 "Grandpa." This modified design pistol is known to collectors as the "Papa" Nambu.

The "Papa" was officially adopted by the Imperial Japanese Navy on September 10, 1909. Curiously, although "Papas" are marked with *kanji* reading "Army Type," the design was never adopted by the Imperial Army. The pistols were available for purchase by Japanese officers, however, and more than 800 were apparently procured specifically for Army service. Although the "Papa" was officially replaced by the Type 14 beginning in 1926, the Japanese military experienced continuing shortages of handguns as the empire expanded, and many "Papas" remained in service through the end of World War II. Unfortunately, this extended and often arduous service life was not very kind to the pistols, and most "Papas" encountered show extensive surface wear, often including rust and pitting. Broken or missing parts are also not unusual. As a result, like the Type 26, "Papas" in fine original condition should be considered rare prizes for the collector.

The "Papa" was produced both by the Tokyo Artillery Arsenal (TAA) and by Tokyo Gas Electric Co., Ltd. (TGE). Two different types of receivers were used, with TAA machining the original design from a single steel forging, while TGE produced a modified design consisting of two bilateral halves pinned and soldered together prior to final machining. To confuse matters, some TGE "Papas" were built on one-piece frames supplied by Tokyo arsenal. The two designs can be distinguished by the fact that Tokyo Arsenal receivers have milled recesses on the flats just to the rear of the top of the grip frame, while TGE receivers have no milled recesses in this area. Production of the "Papa" continued at TAA until 1923, and at TGE until 1928. Estimated total production was 4,600 TAA pistols and 5,700 by TGE.

Serialization of "Papas" produced by Tokyo Artillery Arsenal was a continuation of the original "Grandpa" serial series; the lowest known specimen is serial #2460, while the highest recorded is 7026. TGE initially started a new serial series with number 1, and continued this to 4,999 (serial #4866 is the highest reported in this

Tokyo Arsenal "Papa" Nambu serial number 2827, showing right side type markings and naval anchor. Note milled recess in receiver flat behind top of grip panel. *Courtesy Harry L. Derby III.*

Tokyo Arsenal "Papa" Nambu serial number 2827, showing left side markings. Painted *kanji* numeral on grip panel are unit markings. *Courtesy Harry L. Derby III.*

Tokyo Gas Electric Co. "Papa" Nambu serial number 2150, showing the smooth receiver flat behind top of grip panel found on all TGE-fabricated "Papa" receivers, and the added Tokyo Arsenal symbol found on Tokyo Arsenal Contract TGE variants.

group). For reasons that are unclear, the 5,000, 6,000, and 7,000 serial blocks were not used. A second TGE serial series was begun with 8,001, and probably continued to about 8,700, with the highest reported TGE serial being 8654.

Identification

Superficially, the "Papa" is similar in appearance to the "Grandpa" (see Chapter III), except for the size of the trigger guard, which is 35 mm in diameter, the movable rather than fixed lanyard loop, and the magazine base, which is made of aluminum rather than wood. The "Papa" also carries additional markings on the left side of the receiver, as noted below. There are actually many other minor differences, and most parts are not interchangeable between the two models. The "Papa" is also slightly heavier at 2 lbs, 3 ounces. Although some "Papas" were produced with slots to accommodate shoulder stocks, most examples either lack the stock slot, or have had it filled with soft metal.

Field Disassembly

Follow the procedure described for the "Grandpa" Nambu in Chapter 3.

Markings

"Papa" Nambus carry the same *kanji* markings as the "Grandpa" on the right rear of the receiver, above the serial number. Most "Papas" also have the *kanji* 式陸, reading from right to left, "Army Type" on the left side opposite the serial number. (The only known exceptions are two pistols that were evidently specially prepared as presentation pieces, as noted below.) The top of the chamber on TAA "Papas" is marked with the arsenal symbol, while the chambers of TGE guns are marked with the company logo .

Naval contract pistols produced by TGE also carry naval inspection marks, which were required because they were arms made by a private contractor. Two styles of naval anchors were used for this purpose, labeled as "Type A" (⚓) and "Type B" (⚓). The earliest TGE pistols supplied to the Navy (approximately 75) carry the Type A anchor stamped in the grip safety well. After this point, the naval anchor was moved to a position on the right side of the frame preceding the serial number. The first naval contract was for approximately 1,300 pistols, but during the contract period some pistols were also sold privately; the highest reported "Papa" with a Type A anchor is serial #1852. TGE pistols produced for the second and third naval contracts are marked with Type B anchors. (One out-of-range specimen, serial #680, is also marked with a Type B anchor; it was most probably a pistol that had been retained in inventory for private purchase, but was shifted to the contract in response to declining private sales.) Naval contract pistols may also carry the encircled *kana* syllable *to* (㋣) as a naval inspection mark.

TGE "Papas" procured by the Army also required arsenal approval markings because of their production by a private contractor. Army "Papas," referred to as "Tokyo Arsenal Contract" variants, carry the TAA symbol ( ) stamped on the right side preceding the serial number.

Stocked "Papa"

Although early "Papas" were manufactured with slots for shoulder stocks, most had these slots filled, and were not issued with stocks. Three Thai-contract pistols (serial #4556, 4561, and 4692) have open slots, are accompanied by matching shoulder stocks, and were apparently part of a special order; such pistols are extremely rare. TGE serial #19, accompanied by matching TGE stock #19, carries no "Army Type" markings, and is believed to have been presented as a sales incentive to government officials in Mexico during the negotiation of their Arisaka rifle contract. One specimen, serial #4552, is fitted with a non-standard shoulder stock similar to the stocks accompanying Luger "carbines." This pistol is equipped with a 10.5" fluted barrel, and has other non-standard features, including the absence of the "Army Type' markings as on TGE #19; it was acquired in Japan after the end of World War II by a U.S. Army officer, and was evidently custom made by the factory for a distinguished customer.

Variations

There are two recognized TAA and eight recognized TGE variations of the "Papa." These are identified by external markings and serial number ranges, although, as noted above, occasional out-of-range specimens have been reported. The estimated totals shown below are based on a mathematical analysis of occurrence of known specimens, and provide a reasonable index of relative abundance or scarcity.

Because of their long service lives, much of it as second-class weapons, most "Papas" are in fair to poor condition, commonly showing extensive surface rust and/or pitting and little original finish; broken or missing parts are not unusual, and magazines are more often than not mismatched. For this reason, values of "Papas" are usually more dependent upon condition than on variation, and prices are very difficult to predict with any degree of reliability. Rough specimens generally will bring prices in the $500-$650 range, depending upon individual characteristics, with a significant component of this price being the condition and salvageability of parts, especially the magazine. "Papas" in very good condition, with most of their original finish and no broken or missing parts, will typically bring prices of $1,300 to $1,500, with rare variants increasing this range to as much as $2,000. Truly fine examples are rare, and may bring $5,000 or more, depending upon individual characteristics, and a fine example with an original shoulder stock is in a class with the "Grandpa" and may bring $15,000 or more. Assembling a complete collection of "Papa" variations in fine condition is a daunting challenge.

Variation	Frame Type	Special Markings	Serial Range	Estimated Total
Tokyo Arsenal				**4,600**
Standard Production	1-piece	none	2,450-7,050	4,550
Thailand Contract	1-piece	Thai *Charka*	4,550-4,700	50
Tokyo Gas Electric Co., Ltd.				**5,700**
1st Variation Naval Contract	2-piece	Type A Anchor	1-1,900	1,300
2nd Variation Naval Contract	2-piece	Type B Anchor	2,325-2,700 3,000-4,700	1,570
3rd Variation Naval Contract	1-piece	Type B Anchor	2,700-3,149 8,550-8,700	685
1st Variation Tokyo Arsenal Contract	2-piece	Tokyo Arsenal symbol	700-2,816 (interspersed)	565
2nd Variation Tokyo Arsenal Contract	2-piece	Tokyo Arsenal symbol	1,900-3,000 8,000-8,200	260
8,000 Series Tokyo Arsenal Contract	1-piece	Tokyo Arsenal symbol	8,075-8,549	420
1st Variation Private Purchase	2-piece	none	300-1,900	600
2nd Variation Private Purchase	2-piece	none	1,900-4,999 8,000-8,200	300

The "Papa" was normally equipped with a matching second magazine, a holster with shoulder strap, a braided cotton lanyard with leather slide and keeper, and a cleaning rod. Pistols with shoulder stocks were probably not provided with separate holsters.

While similar in size and general shape, holsters for the "Papa" are readily distinguishable from both those designed for the 1902 "Grandpa," and from those made for the later Type 14. They are made of cowhide leather, with a clamshell closure flap that is secured by a leather strap with a brass keyhole plate mating with a brass stud on the holster body. An ammunition pouch containing loops for 16 cartridges is sewn to the outside of the body under the clamshell, and has a separate closure flap. Two leather blocks are sewn into the inside of the body for stiffening, and provide a separate storage space for the spare magazine. A small leather loop retains the cleaning rod within the same space. Shoulder strap rings are oval and made of brass. Replica "Papa" holsters and straps have recently been imported; these holsters can be distinguished from originals by the rivet pattern on the closure strap latchplate (see illustration, Chapter 5).

"Papa" cleaning rods are uncommon. They are made of nickeled steel, and are 147 mm long, with a 90 degree bend at one end forming a handle 15 mm long. The opposite end is flattened and slotted for a patch, while the tip is formed into a screwdriver blade.

Ammunition for the "Papa" was originally provided in 50-round boxes made of light brown cardboard. Cartridge boxes dated before 1926 and carrying the "Army Type" *kanji* weapon identification as shown below are very rare.

包薬弾•銃拳式陸
發拾五

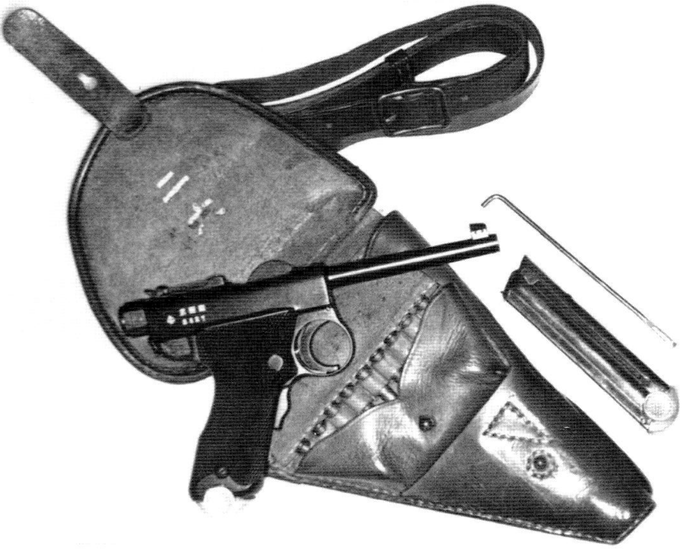

"Papa" Nambu with holster, extra magazine, and cleaning rod. *Courtesy Harry L. Derby III.*

V

The "Baby" Nambu

Perhaps the most highly prized of all Japanese handguns, the Nambu Automatic Pistol Type B, known to collectors as the "Baby" Nambu, was designed concurrently with the 1902 "Grandpa." It was envisioned as a smaller pistol to be carried as a personal weapon by officers (although it was available for private purchase), and was chambered for the unique 7x20 mm Nambu cartridge. Its cost, however, was nearly twice that of a comparable 1910 Browning or 1903 Pocket Model Colt, and sales remained modest. Although the first "Baby" was probably produced in 1903, full manufacture probably began in 1909, and continued until about 1929. The total number produced did not exceed 6,500; the highest standard serial number reported is 6448.

Two manufacturers were involved in "Baby" production. The Tokyo Artillery Arsenal (TAA) produced at least the first 5,900 pistols, and Tokyo Gas Electric Co. (TGE) produced the final group of approximately 550.

Identification

The "Baby" Nambu is a 7 mm semiautomatic pistol with an exposed barrel, fixed sights, a single recoil spring located in a tunnel on the left side of the receiver, a small (20 mm) circular trigger guard, a grip safety located on the front grip strap, a 68-degree angled grip frame, and bordered and checkered walnut grip panels. It has a checkered push-button magazine catch located in the left grip panel behind the trigger, and a fixed lanyard loop located on the rear of the receiver below the cocking knob. It is 172 mm (6.77") in length, and weighs 1 lb 5 oz. Its magazine has a capacity of seven cartridges.

"Baby" Nambu pistols, right and left side views.

Top view of "Baby" Nambu pistols showing Tokyo Arsenal (upper) and Tokyo Gas Electric Co. chamber markings. ("Papa" chambers carry similar manufacturer's markings on their chambers.)

Disassembly

Follow the procedures described for the "Grandpa" Nambu in Chapter 3.

Variations

Three primary variants of the "Baby" are recognized. The first two represent the production of the two manufacturers, TAA and TGE. These are readily identified by the manufacturer's symbol stamped on the top of the chamber, and , respectively. A third rare variant is the "Imperial Gift Baby." All known examples of this variant were produced by TAA, and carry the engraved *kanji* 御 賜 (*ON SHI*, meaning "Imperial Gift") arranged vertically on the top of the barrel extension between the ejection port and the rear sight. Fourteen imperial gift examples are known; all are TAA pistols from the 929-5801 serial range. Any newly found specimens of this variant

Top view of "Imperial Gift Baby" showing added *kanji* markings behind ejection port. *Courtesy Harry L. Derby III.*

should be compared to lists of known standard serial numbers and given expert examination before being accepted as genuine, due to the risk of forgery.

One specimen (serial #613) bearing the encircled *kana* syllable *to* (㋣) has been examined. This character was used as a Naval acceptance mark, and the pistol may have been a test gun purchased by the Navy for evaluation. This cannot be positively confirmed, and the "Baby" was never officially adopted by the Japanese military.

Very early "Babys" have several unique features that were part of the original design, but were not carried over into standard production. While not true prototypes, these early production pistols are nonetheless quite rare, and are of significant interest to advanced collectors. Any "Baby" serialized below #500 should be considered rare, as only six surviving specimens from this serial range are known.

A single out-of-serial-range "Baby" is known, serial #10000. Its condition and the circumstances of its acquisition indicate that it may have been a special order pistol prepared for a distinguished customer.

Two examples are known of "Babys" that have been modified to form the hilt of a military sword. These are known in Japan as *Shisei kenjyu tsuki gunto*, "experimental pistol attached to sword."

Values of "Baby" Nambus vary with production period, manufacturer, condition, special features, and inclusion of the original spare magazine and other accessories. Tokyo Arsenal specimens in very good condition rarely change hands for less than $2,500 today, and fine specimens may bring $3,500. Very early examples (generally with serial numbers below 500) carry a special premium, and values must be judged carefully based on their historic significance. TGE pistols typically bring $2,000 to $2,500 more than equivalent Tokyo Arsenal specimens, and the inclusion of the original matching spare magazine adds $500 to $750 to the value of the pistol alone. Original holsters often command prices of $1,000 or more in very good condition, and original cleaning rods can bring $125 to $200. The rare "Imperial Gift" specimens are seldom offered for sale, and can be expected to bring prices in the $10,000 to $15,000 range. Original 7 mm Nambu cartridges typically sell for $35 to $40; unopened boxes of original ammunition generally bring prices in the $2,000 to $2,500 range.

Accessories

The "Baby" was normally provided with its second matching magazine, a holster with strap, a woven 6 mm diameter cotton lanyard with leather keepers, and a nickeled steel cleaning rod. Leather spare ammunition pouches designed to fit a 50-round box of 7 mm ammunition were also available for purchase.

Original soft-shell (left) and reproduction of rare hard-shell "Baby" Nambu holsters. Note the difference in rivet patterns on the flap closure latchplates; original Japanese holsters of all types with riveted latchplates have the two side rivets positioned closer to the bottom in an "inverted cruciate" pattern.

The earliest "Baby" holsters are ¾ scale models of the standard "Papa" holster made of smooth cowhide leather with a hard clamshell closure flap, a solid leather closure strap with an oval brass latchplate, a mating closure stud mounted on the body, and oval brass attachment loops for the shoulder strap. An ammunition pouch with loops for 14 cartridges is located on the body under the closure flap; a recess for the spare magazine and a retaining loop for the cleaning rod are provided inside the holster body. Original "hard shell" holsters are very rare; at least two commercial reproductions have been produced, and expert examination may be required to distinguish these from the originals, especially if they have been intentionally "aged." The more common "Baby" holster, made of pigskin, has a softer molded closure flap with similar hardware, ammunition pouch, and internal storage arrangements as the "hard shell." A rare variant is similar in design except for the closure strap, which is teardrop shaped and has a keyhole-shaped stud slot that lacks the brass latchplate of the more common model. Some late production "Baby" holsters are made of smooth cowhide rather than pigskin.

Holster straps are either 17 mm or 19 mm wide, and vary from 48" to 56" in length. Strap hardware is made of brass, and the edges of the straps are welted.

Cleaning rods are "L" shaped and are 135mm long, with a 90-degree bend at one end forming a handle 12 mm in length. The end opposite the handle is flattened and slotted to accept a cleaning patch, while the tip is formed into a screwdriver blade. The rods are made of nickeled steel; most, but not all, carry Tokyo Arsenal inspection marks.

Japanese 7x20 mm ammunition was originally packaged in 50-round brown cardboard boxes that are 90x47x29 mm in size. They are marked in *kanji*, "Small Automatic Pistol • Loaded Ammunition / 50 Rounds:"

小型自動拳銃 • 實包
五O發

The first line is arranged in a circle around the arsenal symbol, while the second line is placed horizontally below the circle.

Reproductions of the "Baby" holster and its shoulder strap have recently been imported. They are made of cowhide leather with brass fittings. All of the current reproductions can be identified by the rivet pattern on the closure strap latchplate, which is different from the originals.

VI

The Experimental Mark A Automatic Pistol

The *Shisei Ko Go Jido Kenjyu*, commonly referred to as the "15-Shot Experimental," is a distinctive and much-sought Japanese collector's item. It is also a very rare and valuable pistol. Six examples are known from the serial range 1-14, and as many as 20 may have been produced. The design, by Kijiro Nambu, was a transitional model fabricated in 1920 at the Tokyo Artillery Arsenal in an effort to develop a more advanced pistol than the "Papa" that could also be produced more economically. Although many of its features were dropped in the successive Type 14 design for reasons of economy, the Type 14 contains a number of elements that clearly originated in the "Experimental."

Identification

The Mark A Experimental is an 8 mm semiautomatic pistol with an exposed barrel, an adjustable tangent rear sight, an unusual 55 degree grip angle, a wide receiver with the top of the bolt exposed, and a double-column 15-round nickel plated magazine with an aluminum base. The magazine base has a circular checkered gripping surface on each side. The magazine latch is a button located low on the front grip strap. Grip panels are made of checkered black bakelite, and each panel is retained by a single screw at its lower end. The trigger guard is removable, and a combination safety and dismounting lever is located above it on the left side. The rear of the bolt is formed into a wide finger-grooved cocking piece, and the bolt is retained in the receiver by a transverse crossbolt inserted from the right side. The pistol is 255 mm (10.04") in length and weighs 2 lbs. 7 oz unloaded. The barrel extension has one milled horizontal weight reducing channel on the left side and two channels on the right; the bolt has two longitudinal weight reducing channels milled in the rear portion of its upper surface. Exterior markings are absent except for the serial number, which is generally stamped into the lower end of the trigger guard on the right side. Some specimens also have the *kanji* 二 (*NI*, the numeral 2) stamped on the rear of the cocking knob, indicating a "second class" weapon, not for military issue.

Because of their scarcity and attractiveness to collectors, establishing values for the Mark A Experimental is on a case-by-case basis. The last two known sales were reportedly in the $25,000 to $30,000 range.

Accessories

A boxy, triangular shaped cowhide holster was prepared for the Mark A Experimental; it has a shoulder strap and internal storage space for a spare magazine. Only one example is known. A matching second magazine was also provided for each pistol.

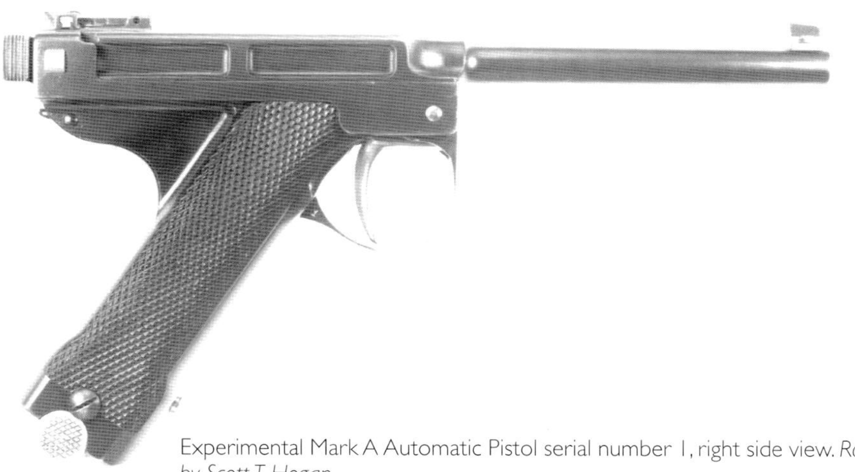

Experimental Mark A Automatic Pistol serial number 1, right side view. *Robert E. Hogan Collection, photo by Scott T. Hogan.*

VII

The Type 14

The Type 14 is the most common and widely recognized of all Japanese handguns. Approximately 279,000 pistols of this type were produced by five manufacturers in the period from 1926 through 1945.

The type designation is based on the year of its adoption, 1925, which was the 14th year of the *Taisho* Era.

With the adoption of the Type 14, Japan instituted the practice of stamping the era year and month of manufacture on each pistol. This is of great significance to both historians and collectors, as it not only allows the tracing of the pistols' production histories, but it also creates an instant array of variations based on these dates. This, combined with the number of manufacturers and the series of design changes that occurred during 20 years of Type 14 production, provides a range of variations that probably surpasses any other collectible military firearm. This variety is so large that to date no collector has assembled a truly complete collection of Type 14s by dates, to say nothing of the many other variations.

Early (upper, Nagoya-Chigusa factory serial number 872 made in July 1927) and late (lower, Nagoya-Toriimatsu factory second series serial number 71847 made in June 1945) examples of the Type 14. Note smooth "slab" grip panels on the late production example, used beginning in November 1944.

The original Type 14 design included no provision for a magazine safety, and used a striker design that proved unsatisfactory under the severe winter conditions encountered in Manchuria. As a result, previously issued pistols were recalled beginning in 1932 (*Showa* 7) for modification, and pistols produced in and after 1932 onward incorporated the magazine safety and revised striker and spring guide. Some pistols, however, were missed by the recall, and are a rare class of early production variants that are described below.

The exterior finishing treatment of the Type 14 follows an interesting progression. The earliest pistols produced show very good quality workmanship, but attention to their finishing could still be called "utilitarian." The introduction of potential competition between the Nagoya and Tokyo Arsenals in mid-1928 (*Showa* 3) resulted in a gradual improvement in surface treatment quality by both manufacturers. When Kijiro Nambu's private Kokubunji factory began production in late 1933 (*Showa* 8), exterior polishing and rust blueing approached the best commercial standards. This level of quality was generally maintained until 1940 (*Showa* 15), when growing wartime production pressures gradually forced a relaxation of quality standards. When Toriimatsu factory production was initiated in late 1941 (*Showa* 16), the finishing standard had again returned to the "utilitarian" level. During wartime production, both the Kokubunji and Toriimatsu factories exhibited a gradual decline in exterior machining standards. The Kokubunji factory continued to apply some cosmetic surface buffing, and used heat "strawing" on triggers. It also ignored the production expedients introduced at the Toriimatsu factory until its Type 14 production ended in August 1944 (*Showa* 19.8). Exterior treatment quality of Toriimatsu pistols slowly declined until the end of 1944, when marked improvements were implemented. These improvements were maintained until late June 1945 (*Showa* 20.6), when organized production collapsed. Type 14 assembly continued until early August (*Showa* 20.8) without formal inspection, and with both mechanical and finishing results that range from "crude and dangerous" to "surprisingly good." The study of these "Last Ditch" specimens is fascinating, and they are prized by specialized collectors.

Identification

The Type 14 is an 8 mm semiautomatic pistol with a 117 mm (4.6") exposed barrel, fixed sights, a 65 degree grip, horizontally serrated or smooth wooden panels, and a grooved aluminum or aluminum alloy magazine base. It has dual internal recoil springs riding in channels located on each side of the bolt and barrel extension. It may have either a round or a horizontally elongated trigger guard that is removable from the receiver. A knurled cocking knob of either a grooved or solid cylindrical design is mounted on the end of the bolt at the pistol's rear. The safety is a rotary lever mounted forward on the left side of the receiver; a knurled button-type magazine catch is located in a hole in the left grip panel behind the trigger. A fixed lanyard loop is mounted on the rear of the receiver above the grip frame. The pistol is 231 mm (9.1") in length, weighs 2 lbs, and has a magazine capacity of eight cartridges.

Field Disassembly

Clear the pistol by removing the magazine and making sure it is empty, pulling the cocking knob approximately ½" to the rear (do not fully cock it), and inspecting the rear of the chamber to ensure that it is not loaded. Replace the magazine, pull the trigger to make sure that the striker is uncocked, and again remove the magazine.

Push the end of the striker spring guide, located in the center of the cocking knob, all the way in, and while holding it in this position, rotate the cocking knob counter-clockwise until it can be removed from the bolt. Remove the striker spring and guide from the rear of the bolt.

Place the pistol's muzzle against a firm surface and push it in until the barrel extension moves approximately ¼" to the rear. While holding it in this position, push the magazine catch in as far as it will go, and pull the trigger guard downward approximately ½". (NOTE: If the trigger guard will not move, stop. Remove the grip panel screws, lift the bottoms of the grip panels, and remove them from the grip frame. Tight grip panels may be damaged by removing the trigger guard.)

Slide the barrel assembly forward out of the receiver. Remove the locking block from the bottom of the barrel extension; slide the bolt and recoil springs out of the rear of the barrel extension, and remove the striker from the rear of the bolt.

If you have not already done so, remove the left grip panel. Push in on the magazine catch, slide the trigger guard all the way out of engagement with the receiver, and remove the magazine catch and its spring from their recess.

Visually inspect the locking block spring, located in a horizontal recess in the upper rear of the magazine well, from the top of the receiver. It should be retained in place by tension of its rear coil against the inside of the recess, but if is loose, it may fall out and become lost.

Reassemble the pistol in reverse order. When inserting the barrel assembly into the receiver, turn the pistol upside down so that the locking block remains in the "locked" position during the process. In reassembling the striker spring guide and cocking knob, the lug on the bottom of the guide must fit into the slot in the bottom of the bolt; screw the knob all the way in until it stops, then release the guide and unscrew the knob slowly until the guide snaps into place, locking the knob.

Primary External Markings

The external markings on the Type 14 are categorized on the basis of their location and significance. The left side of the receiver carries the type *kanji* 十四年式 in 4 mm characters stamped on the rear of the flat below the bridge; these read, from left to right, "Fourteen Year Type." The *kanji* for "fire" (火) and "safe" (安) are stamped as 4 mm characters just outside of the safety lever's arc of rotation, to the front and rear of the lever itself, respectively. On all but a relatively small number of early pistols, a double-ended semicircular arrow is stamped above the safety lever to indicate that it should be rotated through its upper quadrant when changing the lever's position to avoid damaging the left grip panel.

On the right side of the receiver, there are two lines of markings that are 3.0 mm to 4.5 mm in height. The upper line consists of up to three symbols indicating the manufacturer and, if applicable, serial series, followed by up to five serial digits. The lower line is the era date of manufacture, consisting of the year followed by the month, separated by either a comma or a period. In 1930 the *kanji* 昭 (*SHO*, for *Showa*) was added preceding the date.

The meanings of the arsenal, factory, series, and date prefix symbols are as follows:

- [symbol] Nagoya Arsenal
- [symbol] Tokyo and Kokura Arsenals
- [symbol] Nambu Rifle Mfg. Co. (later Chuo Kogyo Co., Ltd.), Kokubunji factory
- ㋑ First serial series (after the original)
- ㋺ Second serial series (after the original)
- 昭 *Showa* Era identifier (*SHO*), added in 1930 (*Showa* 5, 6 to Nagoya Arsenal pistols and *Showa* 5.10-5.11 to Tokyo Arsenal pistols); several different forms of this character were used.

Serial Series

When Type 14 production began at Nagoya Arsenal in 1926 and Tokyo Arsenals in 1928 (*Taisho* 15 and *Showa* 2, respectively), each used its own serial series starting with serial #1. It was probably assumed that arsenal markings were adequate to differentiate between the two series, and the Japanese probably did not then envision the number of Type 14s that would ultimately be produced. (Total production of all models of Japanese cartridge handguns before the introduction of the Type 14 did not exceed 79,000.) In 1935 (*Showa* 10), with its military production expanding in conjunction with its pursuit of an empire, the Japanese adopted a serialization system for firearms that limited serial numbers to five digits. Once a series of serial numbers reached 99,999, a new series was begun with serial #1, preceded by an encircled *kana* character as an identifier. The order of *kana* assignment follows the arrangement of the poem *Iroha*, the traditional Japanese syllabary. As used by the Japanese, the "original" series carries no identifier; the first series after the original (referred to as the "first series") carries the encircled *kana* "*i*" (pronounced "*ee*"), and the second series after the original carries the encircled *kana* "*ro*." Some collectors refer to the "*i*" and "*ro*" series as "A" and "B," or "First" and "Second," respectively.

The original serial series initiated by the Nagoya Chigusa factory in 1926 had reached approximately serial #7,830 when Nagoya production ended in November 1932 (*Showa* 7.11). The separate Tokyo Arsenal series remained continuous when Tokyo production was moved to Kokura Arsenal; it had reached approximately serial #35,425 by the time Kokura production ended in June 1936 (*Showa* 11.6). When Nambu's Kokubunji factory began Type 14 production in December 1933 (*Showa* 8.12) under Nagoya Arsenal supervision, it continued the original Nagoya serial series, starting at approximately serial #7,830. This series was continued until serial #99,999 was reached in October 1941 (*Showa* 16.10).

At this time, the Toriimatsu factory of Nagoya Arsenal was preparing to initiate production of the Type 14. A decision was made to start the new "*i*" (first) series with serial #1 at the Kokubunji factory, while Toriimatsu was assigned the "*i*" series serial block beginning with #50,001. Kokubunji production never reached the end of its assigned first series serial block, but Toriimatsu reached first series serial #99,999 in November 1943 (*Showa* 18.11), and began a second series the same month. Second series Toriimatsu production had reached the low 73,000 serial range when operations ended in August 1945.

External Inspection Marks

In addition to the arsenal, series, serial number, and date markings, there are small (usually 1.5 to 2 mm) inspection marks in various locations on the Type 14 that can be extremely significant to the pistol's identification. In order to facilitate discussion, the most important locations for the placement of these marks have been labeled as follows:

"A" Position marks are located on the right side of the receiver adjacent to the date, and generally below it or to its right. These marks signify the final approval of the supervisory arsenal inspector. In some cases, this defines the arsenal to which the pistol's production is credited.

"B" Position marks are located on the left side of the receiver near the center of the flat immediately behind the top of the grip panel. One or more of these marks generally are found on Type 14s dated before *Showa* 7, and they are rarely also found on later dated pistols. They represent arsenal repair or rebuilding work, and in most cases identify the arsenal that performed the bolt and receiver modifications to install the revised striker and new magazine safety during the 1932-40 recall program.

"C" Position marks are located on the left side of the receiver at the rear of the same panel that carries the "B" position marks, but to the edge of the panel adjacent to the lanyard loop. These marks were used only by the Tokyo and Kokura Arsenals, and represent a factory assembly inspection apparently conducted prior to the final arsenal supervisor's inspection. These marks distinguish pistols assembled at Kokura Arsenal from those assembled at Tokyo Arsenal.

"D" Position marks are located on the rear flat of the receiver, against which the cocking knob rests when the bolt is closed. They are generally stamped near the lower right corner of the flat, at four to five o'clock relative to the circle of the cocking knob, but they have also been observed on the left side of the flat above the sear bar recess. These marks are believed to be the "signature" of a single inspector in the Tokyo Arsenal system. He apparently was assigned to the regular Tokyo Arsenal inspection staff in early 1934 (*Showa* 9), but was detailed, at least briefly during this period, to the Tokyo Arsenal inspection office in the Kokubunji factory. After finishing 1934 at Tokyo Arsenal, he was apparently transferred permanently to the Kokubunji inspection office when Type 14 production was shifted to Kokura in early 1935. He continued as the principle inspector of Type 14 frames until either being promoted or leaving the factory in May or June 1939 (*Showa* 14.5 – 14.6). While this explanation involves a significant amount of conjecture, the significance of "D" position marks is that they provide interesting evidence of the transfer of frames from the Tokyo Arsenal, and later from the Kokubunji factory, to the Kokura Arsenal.

Other frame marking positions include the lower edges of the front and rear grip straps (under the panels) used by all manufacturers for frame inspections, and a location on the left side of the frame just below the magazine catch opening, used exclusively by the Toriimatsu factory for frame inspections.

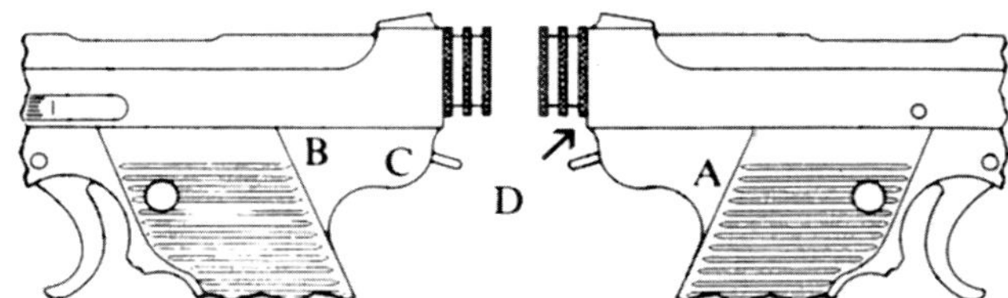

Type 14 Frame Marking Positions

Examples of Type 14 Arsenal, Serial, Date, and "A" Inspection Markings

The following are examples of right-side receiver markings from each of the Type 14 manufacturers, showing typical patterns and changes over time. Inspection marks are shown to the right of the date to conserve space, but in actual practice they may appear above, below, or to the right of the date. Text to the right of the markings indicates the proper interpretation of their meaning.

• **Nagoya Arsenal, Chigusa factory:** Early Nagoya Arsenal Type 14s carry an arsenal symbol that is small (initially 2.5 mm in diameter), and precedes the date rather than the serial number. The size of the symbol was increased to 3.5 mm in 1928 (*Showa* 3). In 1929 (*Showa* 4) it was again increased in size to 4 mm, and was moved to a position to the left of the serial number, while the *SHO* (昭) character was added to the left of the date. With one notable exception the Nagoya Arsenal symbol, used alone, indicates the Chigusa factory of Nagoya Arsenal, which produced the Type 14 from late 1926 through late 1932. (The exception is a small group of the earliest Kokubunji factory Type 14s dated *Showa* 8.12—see text below.) Chigusa factory pistols can also be identified by the use of a comma rather than a decimal to separate the year and month in the date.

71 ⊗ 15,12 門田	Nagoya Arsenal Chigusa factory original series serial #71 1926, December (*Taisho* Era, small arsenal symbol))
872 ⊗ 2,7 門田	Nagoya Arsenal Chigusa factory original series serial #872 1927, July (*Showa* Era, small arsenal symbol)
4168 ⊗ 4,2 筒門	Nagoya Arsenal Chigusa factory original series serial #4168 1928, February (intermediate arsenal symbol)
⊗ 7309 昭 7,4 平山	Nagoya Arsenal Chigusa factory original series serial #7309 1932, April (large arsenal symbol, added *SHO*)

• **Nagoya Arsenal, Toriimatsu factory:** With the exception of a very small number of 1939 (*Showa* 14)-dated pre-production guns, Type 14s manufactured by the Nagoya Arsenal's Toriimatsu factory always carry a serial series identifier (⊘ or ⊜) between the Nagoya Arsenal symbol and the serial number. *Showa* dates, which range from October 1941 through August 1945 (*Showa* 16.10 to 20.8) have the year and month separated by a period, and the "A" position supervisory inspection mark (if present) is always the Nagoya Arsenal supervisory mark *NA* (名).

00 ⊗ ⊘ 50006 昭 16.12 名	"second class weapon" Nagoya Arsenal Toriimatsu factory first series serial #50006, 1941, December
⊗ ⊘ 67034 昭 18.2 名	Nagoya Arsenal Toriimatsu factory first series serial #67034, 1943, February
⊗ ⊜ 2999 昭 18.11 名	Nagoya Arsenal Toriimatsu factory second series serial #2999, 1943, November
⊗ ⊜ 71847 昭 20.6 名	Nagoya Arsenal Toriimatsu factory second series serial #71847, 1945, June
⊗ ⊜ 72922 昭 20.8	Nagoya Arsenal Toriimatsu factory second series serial #72922, 1945, August (no inspection)

• **Tokyo and Kokura Arsenals:** Production of the Type 14 began at the Tokyo Arsenal in May 1928 (*Showa* 3.5). In late 1932 (*Showa* 7) the assembly operation was moved to Kokura Arsenal, although Tokyo continued to fabricate frames and parts, and retained inspection authority until November 1934 (*Showa* 9.11). In that month Kokura began to assume its own inspection authority. A transitional period evidently occurred between November 1934 and February or March 1935 (*Showa* 10.2 – 10.3), after which all duties were assumed by Kokura. When the Tokyo/Kokura Arsenal symbol is accompanied by any "A" position inspection mark *other than* 幡 (*HATA*) or 小 (*KO*), and any "C" position mark *other than* セ (*se*), the pistol was produced by Tokyo Arsenal. When the arsenal symbol is accompanied by any "A" position inspection mark *other than* 幡 or 小 and the "C" position mark is セ, the pistol was assembled at Kokura Arsenal under Tokyo Arsenal supervision. When the arsenal symbol is accompanied by either the 幡 or 小 inspection mark in the "A" position, the pistol was produced by Kokura Arsenal under its own supervisory authority.

♧ 281 3.6	Tokyo Arsenal serial #281 1928, June
♧ 16497 5.10	Tokyo Arsenal serial #16497 1930, October
♧ 16610 昭 5.11	Tokyo Arsenal serial #16610 1930, November (added *SHO*)
♧ 25981 昭 8.2 東	Tokyo Arsenal (Kokura Assembly) serial #25981 1933, February (*TO* inspection, with *se* "C" position mark on left side)
♧ 29888 昭 9.11 幡	Kokura Arsenal (transition) serial #29888 1934, November (*HATA* inspection, with *se* "C" position mark on left side)
♧ 32696 昭 10.6 小	Kokura Arsenal serial #32696 1935, June (*KO* inspection, with *se* "C" position mark on left side)

• **Nambu Kokubunji factory:** Type 14 production at the Kokubunji factory of the Nambu Rifle Manufacturing Co. began in December 1933 under Nagoya Arsenal supervision, continuing the original Nagoya Arsenal serial series. When accompanied by the Nambu (later merged into Chuo Kogyo Kabushikigaisha, or Chuo Kogyo Co., Ltd.) Kokubunji factory symbol, either alone or with the first serial series symbol, the Nagoya Arsenal symbol indicates arsenal supervisory authority over the civilian factory. Although the supervisory authority over the Kokubunji factory rested with the Nagoya Arsenal, the actual inspection office was staffed by Tokyo Arsenal personnel, and inspection marks used at Kokubunji throughout the production of the Type 14 are associated with Tokyo Arsenal.

As noted above, a small number of pistols produced during the start-up period at Kokubunji carry no factory symbol; these can be distinguished from late Nagoya Arsenal production by their dates, and by the use of periods rather than commas to separate the year and month. The Kokubunji factory symbol was initially placed directly below the arsenal symbol, but was moved to a position immediately following the arsenal symbol in February 1934 (*Showa* 9.2), where it remained for the balance of production.

[symbol]7895 昭 8.12 東	Nambu Rifle Mfg. Co. Kokubunji factory early original series serial #7895, 1933, December
[symbol]7993 [symbol] 昭 8.12 東	Nambu Rifle Mfg. Co. Kokubunji factory original series serial #7993 vertical symbol position 1933, December
[symbol][symbol] 8582 昭 9.2 東	Nambu Rifle Mfg. Co. Kokubunji factory original series serial #8582, 1934, February
[symbol][symbol] 17169 昭 11.3 條	Nambu Rifle Mfg. Co. Kokubunji factory original series serial #17169, 1936, March (*Jujyo* inspection used in 1935-1936 only)
[symbol][symbol] 39030 昭 12.11 東	Chuo Kogyo Co. Ltd. Kokubunji factory original series serial #39030, 1937, November
[symbol][symbol][symbol] 33 昭 16.10 東	Chuo Kogyo Co. Ltd. Kokubunji factory first series serial #33, 1941, October
[symbol][symbol][symbol] 20121 昭 19.7 東	Chuo Kogyo Co. Ltd. Kokubunji factory first series serial #20121, 1944, July

Internal Parts Inspection and Serialization

Small parts were examined as they were fabricated, and in most cases they were given an inspection mark to signify that they met dimensional standards. The mark applied was usually the primary one in use by the controlling arsenal at the time, but some marks were specific to individual inspectors. (Inspection marks used before 1932 were derived from the inspectors' names. Beginning in 1932, marks derived from arsenal facilities, e.g *NA* for Nagoya Arsenal and *TO* for Tokyo Arsenal, were phased in, and were used almost exclusively after 1935.) In addition, major parts that required functional testing after fitting (e.g. bolts and barrel extensions) received one or more separate inspection marks to indicate passage of these tests. In some cases these internal marks are very useful in determining the production history of a specific pistol.

Following final fitting, most parts were serialized with up to three digits of the pistol's serial number. In most cases, this was done with the same dies on all parts, including the magazine components, although in early production years smaller sized dies were sometimes used for some parts. (This is not an absolute truism, but it is surprisingly consistent.) In most cases, this makes it possible for the collector to examine magazine and internal parts numbering and, by comparing size, style, and minor imperfections in the numbers with a 10X lens, determine whether or not all parts are original to the gun. In some instances, internal parts markings may be important for variant identification.

"Overlapping" and Out-of-Sequence Dates

One of the incidental effects of the dating of Type 14s is that it establishes a linkage between production dates and specific manufacturing changes and serial number blocks. When an individual pistol has characteristics or a serial number that do not fit the expected pattern, the anomaly raises questions as to its production date.

"Overlapping" refers to the apparent phasing of a change over a period of time, or over a wider than expected range of serial numbers. It is evident with most changes to the Type 14, and results from the Japanese system of parts manufacture and pistol assembly. As parts were fabricated and inspected, they were fed into bins containing similar parts. As these bins were filled they were moved to the assembly line, where each worker picked out parts as needed for the pistol he was fitting and assembling, probably using a tray to hold each pistol's components until it was ready for finishing and final assembly. Several bins for each type of part were undoubtedly used to keep the process moving, and when a change was made, unless it created an incompatibility among the parts being assembled, "new" parts would be placed on top of "old" parts as a bin was filled. Since the rule of "first in, last out" applies to this type of operation, it was inevitable that some of the new parts were incorporated into pistols before all of the old ones were used up, creating the overlapping effect.

The reasons for out-of-sequence dates are not as clear, and may actually be the result of several different events. There is evidence that pistols were occasionally pulled out of the production line prior to final inspection, possibly for special testing and quality control purposes. Since the serial numbers were assigned prior to assembly while dating was done at the time of final inspection and acceptance, such a pistol might well have its dating delayed for a month or more. In addition, problems may have come to light during the assembly process that required a frame or other major component to have additional work performed on it before assembly could be completed. Such "problem" pistols may have been set aside until a specialist had time to attend to them. Whatever the cause, such delays in completing individual pistols evidently occurred during the entire production period, although they become more common after 1942 (*Showa* 17).

Variations

Type 14 variations are best understood if categorized by manufacturer. Of course, collecting Type 14s by manufacturer is itself the objective of many collectors, and represents a worthy objective. However, the Type 14 offers a great deal more territory into which the more adventurous collector may advance.

Nagoya Arsenal, Chigusa factory

• ***Taisho* Era production:** The earliest Type 14s produced by the Nagoya Chigusa factory carry *Taisho* Era dates. Approximately 112 Type 14s were produced in late 1926 (*Taisho* 15). Known examples carry 15,11 and 15,12 dates, but no pistols below serial #42 have been reported. It is believed, based on dates of reported specimens, that production actually began in September or October 1926 (*Taisho* 15,9 or 15,10). All *Taisho* Era pistols are prized by collectors as rare early production specimens, and additional very early examples would be of great interest.

• **"2-dates":** Type 14s produced in 1927 (*Showa* 2) are not especially rare compared to other Nagoya-Chigusa pistols, but they continue to capture collector attention as examples of early Type 14 production, and remain much in demand. (There are no *Showa* 1 dated Type 14s. This is because the *Showa* Era began with the death of Emperor Taisho on December 25, 1926, and its first year, as counted under the Japanese era system, lasted only through December 31. These seven days would have been occupied by the traditional mourning period for Emperor Taisho and preparations for the New Year's celebration; the arsenal thus would not have operated during this period. The first era year was also given a special name by the Japanese (*gannen*), and would have been indicated by the *kanji* 元年, rather than the numeral 1.) Most early Chigusa pistols also lack safety directional arrows. While of interest to some collectors, this does not command an extra premium.

• **Unmodified early production examples:** The original Type 14 design included an 86 mm striker and no provision for a magazine safety. Problems with congealed oil and weak striker fall during cold weather, plus an evident rash of accidental discharges from pistols that were thought to be unloaded when their magazines were removed, led to design changes and a general recall to modify earlier pistols beginning in 1932 (*Showa* 7). A small number of pistols were not returned to the arsenals for modification, and retain their original configuration. They are rare (only 8 Nagoya examples are known), but they are not as widely sought after by collectors as are other variants of similar scarcity.

• **Chigusa inspection marking variants:** At least ten "A" position inspection marks were used by the Chigusa factory during its seven-year production period, always appearing in pairs. Although little interest in this area has been expressed by collectors in the past, recent work to identify and name these marks may increase the demand for the rarer variants. The following marks have been recorded, although serial ranges and periods of occurrence are often broad estimates due to the size and number of gaps between observations.

"A" Position Mark	Reading	Dates of Occurrence	Observed Serial Range
門	*MON*	*Taisho* 15,11-*Showa* 4,2	42-4168
田	*TA*	*Taisho* 15,11-*Showa* 3,3	43-2297
筒	*TSUTSU*	*Showa* 3,4-4,7	2344-4625
河	*KAWA*	*Showa* 4,10-5,4	4837-5382
達	*TATSU*	*Showa* 5,6-6,3	5727-6687
平	*HEI*	*Showa* 4,6-7,4	4528-7327
山	*YAMA*	*Showa* 6,11-7,5	6999-7439
安	*AN*	*Showa* 7,5-7.6	7385-7485
名	*NA*	*Showa* 7,6-7,11	7385-7791
チ	*CHI*	*Showa* 7,7-7,9	7571-7674

• **Other Chigusa date variants:** Type 14 production at the Chigusa factory was never very high, and all year variants are scarce. *Showa* Era Chigusa factory production by year is estimated to be:

1927	1928	1929	1930	1931	1932
(*Showa* 2)	(*Showa* 3)	(*Showa* 4)	(*Showa* 5)	(*Showa* 6)	(*Showa* 7)
1,589	2,130	1,258	1,336	640	757

• **Large trigger guard retrofitting:** After the introduction of the large trigger guard in 1939 (*Showa* 14.9), some earlier pistols were returned to the Kokubunji factory by their owners for replacement of the original guard with the revised design. Some of these pistols also had the magazine retainer spring added to the front strap, with a corresponding notch cut in the front of the magazine. Arsenal-replaced guards are numbered to the gun, and usually carry Kokubunji factory inspection marks; arsenal-modified pistols will also carry a "B" position inspection mark indicating approval of the work. Occasionally, pistols are encountered that have evidently had the original trigger guard replaced by a forward ordnance de-

Examples of Tokyo Arsenal (upper) and Kokura Arsenal Type 14s. Note the pronounced flat ring on the outside of the magazine gripping surface on the Kokura pistol, unique to Kokura produced magazines. Identification of the pistol manufacturer, however, must be determined from inspection marks.

pot and lack "B" position inspection markings. All of these pistols are rare variants.

Tokyo and Kokura Arsenals

• **Unmodified early production:** As with early Nagoya Type 14s, a small number of pistols were not returned for rebuilding during the 1932-40 recall. There are 4 known Tokyo examples of this variant.

• **Arsenal production and assembly variants:** Tokyo Arsenal production of the Type 14 began in *Showa* 3.5, and continued through about *Showa* 7.6. By *Showa* 7.8, pistol assembly had been shifted to Kokura Arsenal, although frames and some other parts evidently continued to be fabricated by Tokyo Arsenal, and Tokyo retained control over the inspection process for some time. In *Showa* 9.11, Kokura Arsenal began to assume full production and inspection authority, although some Tokyo inspection of completed pistols continued into early 1935. By the end of January 1935, all Type 14 production authority had been transferred to Kokura, although pistols continued to be built on surplus Tokyo receivers passed down to Kokura. This sequence of events produced four identifiable production variants: Tokyo production, Tokyo-controlled Kokura assembly, Kokura transition, and Kokura production. These variants can be conclusively identified only through verification of their inspection marks. Data estimates for these variations are as follows:

	Tokyo Production	**Tokyo-controlled Kokura assembly**	**Kokura Transition**	**Kokura Production**
Showa Date range	3.5-7.8	7.8-10.1	9.11-10.1	10.1-11.6
Known Serial range	1-24958	25197-30982	29624-30631	30888-35415
"A" inspection marks	亦 良 貞 南 吾 河 岳 東	東	幡	小
"C" inspection marks	none, 三, 吉 因大	セ	セ	セ
Estimated number	25,420	4,700	1,800	3,500

• **"Kokubunji hybrids":** During the final months of Kokura production in 1936, the Kokubunji factory evidently supplemented Kokura production by providing receivers to make up for the depleted stock passed down from Tokyo Arsenal, although why existing Kokura-fabricated were not used is not known. These pistols can be identified only by the presence of *JYO* (條) or *SHI* (志) "D" position marks on the receiver. To date, only four examples are known, dated *Showa* 11.5 and 11.6.

• **"Pure Kokura" Type 14s:** Only one example of this variant (assembled with Kokura parts on a Kokura-fabricated receiver) has been identified to date, *Showa* 8.9 serial #26323. Identification of this variant is based on the *se* (セ) inspection mark located on the left side of the rear grip strap, indicating fabrication by Kokura Arsenal. (All other Kokura-assembled Type 14s examined are built on Tokyo-fabricated receivers, although it is quite likely that other examples of this variant exist, but have simply not been detected.) Five other receivers fabricated by Kokura Arsenal are known; all are :in-the-white," and lack type and safety *kanji*. Four are unserialized, and were collected from the Toriimatsu factory production line after the end of the war—incomplete, but accompanied by parts made by the Kokubunji factory in 1936. These are believed to have come from depot repair kits assembled by Kokubunji shortly after the close of the Kokura Type 14 production line; they were evidently intended for use by forward ordnance depots for major repairs of damaged pistols. The one serialized example, #32207, is believed to be a "shop" gun assembled at the Kokubunji factory in 1937, with non-standard experimental features. The existence of receivers fabricated by Kokura indicates that a number of complete pistols were probably built on them.

• **Production year variants:** The early years of the 1932-40 recall were low production years for Tokyo Arsenal because of involvement in the rebuilding effort. Production was also low after the final transfer from Tokyo to Kokura. Estimated annual production figures for both arsenals were:

1928	**1929**	**1930**	**1931**	**1932**	**1933**
(*Showa* 3)	(*Showa* 4)	(*Showa* 5)	(*Showa* 6)	(*Showa* 7)	(*Showa* 8)
2,165	6,917	8,751	4,843	3,098	1,125
1934	**1935**	**1936**			
(*Showa* 9)	(*Showa* 10)	(*Showa* 11)			
3,808	4,110	603			

• **"D" marked variants:** Most Tokyo and Kokura Type 14s produced after early *Showa* 9 carry *to* (ト) or *TO* (東) inspection marks in the "D" position. Although the occurrence of these marks is of interest, they do not add a premium to individual pistol values. ("Kokubunji hybrids" are a subset of this group.)

• **Tokyo Arsenal inspection marking variants:** At least eight supervisory ("A") inspection marks were used by the Tokyo Arsenal, and two by the Kokura Arsenal, during their nine years of Type 14 production. In addition, these arsenals used the "C" marking position for factory assembly inspection prior to final arsenal supervisory approval. To date, collectors have shown little interest in the variants produced by these marks, but some are quite rare, and may stimulate further interest as the subject matter becomes better known.

"A" Position Mark	Reading	Observed *Showa* Dates	Observed Serial Range	Estimated Number
菅	*SUGA* (stylized)	3.5-3.9	1-959	1,000
貞	*SADA* (stylized)	3.9-4.7	1063-5040	4,000
貞	*SADA*	4.8-5.6	5751-13439	7,700
本	*HON* (stylized)	5.6-5.9	13524-15345	2,000
吾	S1*	5.10-6.4	16408-20109	4,800
吾	S1*	7.5	24521	100 (?)
河	*KAWA* (stylized)	6.5-6.7	20735-21825	1,500
永	*NAGAI* (stylized)	6.10-7.1	22625-23744	1,300
東	*TO*	7.1-10.1	22965-30982	6,000
幡	*HATA*	9.11-9.12	29624-30631	1,000
小	*KO*	10.1-11.6	30888-35415	5,200

*Labeled as a "symbol"; actual reading unknown

There are six "C" marking variants:

"C" Position Mark	Reading	Observed *Showa* Dates	Observed Serial Range
(none)	(none)	3.5-3.6	1-132
吉	1st *YOSHI*	3.7	548 **(rare)**
三	*MI*	3.6-3.10	281-1492
吉	2nd *YOSHI*	3.11-5.5	1857-12598
内	*UCHI*	5.5-7.5	12965-24521
大	*DAI*	7.8	24958 **(rare)**
セ	*se*	7.8-11.6	25197-36250

• **Large trigger guard retrofitting:** As with Nagoya-Chigusa production, a relatively small number of early Tokyo Type 14s were returned to the arsenal after the introduction of the large trigger guard to have this modification applied to their pistols. This work was generally done by the Kokubunji factory, and the trigger guard will be serialized to the pistol, and usually also carries a *TO* (東) or N inspection mark. An inspection mark in the "B" position was also generally applied to note final approval of the work. Some pistols with replacement large trigger guards also have added magazine retainer springs installed in the front grip strap, while others do not. These pistols are scarce, and are of interest to advanced collectors.

• **"Tokyo Hybrids":** During the first years of the 1932-40 rebuilding program, Tokyo Arsenal apparently received a number of pistols that had been damaged in service, and rebuilt these pistols on new Tokyo receivers. The evidence of this is anecdotal, and not confirmed by factory records, but during the low production years of 1932 and 1933 (*Showa* 7 and 8), a surprising proportion of surviving specimens have "top halves"—barrel extensions, bolts, and usually cocking knobs—that carry numbers and inspection marks from different pistols, sometimes produced by Nagoya Arsenal, and always from the period preceding the receiver date. Although these pistols have previously been regarded as "mismatched," it appears that they are actually factory-assembled "hybrids." Examples are *Showa* 8.2 serial #25981 with Nagoya top half 577 and *Showa* 8.4 serial #26097 with Tokyo top half 491.

• **Prototypes and factory-use pistols:** One Tokyo Type 14 specially modified for ammunition pressure testing has been identified. No Tokyo Arsenal prototypes or cut-away pistols are known.

Kokubunji factory of Nambu Rifle Mfg. Co./Chuo Kogyo Kabushikigaisha, under Nagoya Arsenal supervision

• **"Nagoya Only" markings:** The first Type 14s produced by the Kokubunji factory carry only the Nagoya Arsenal identification symbol. Because Kokubunji production continued the original Nagoya serial series, there have been some questions raised over whether these guns were actually produced at Nagoya or at Kokubunji. However, specific characteristics, including the style of the *SHO* (昭) character and the serial and date numerals demonstrate that they are Kokubunji products. They are very rare; an estimated 75 were produced in December 1933, and only three specimens are known.

• **"Vertical" markings:** Shortly after production began at Kokubunji the factory symbol was added. Initially, the arrangement of the Nagoya and Kokubunji symbols was vertical, with the arsenal symbol above that of the factory. An estimated 425 "verticals" were produced, of which 19 have been reported from the *Showa* 8.12-9.2 date range. They are much sought after by collectors.

• **"D" marked variants:** Two Kokubunji specimens are known from early 1934 (*Showa* 9) that carry *to* (ト) marks in the "D" position. Beginning in 1935 (*Showa* 10) and continuing through mid-1939 (*Showa* 14), the "D" marks become normal, with *SHI* (志) and *JYO* (條) being used during the 1935-36 (*Showa* 10 - 11) Kokura production period, shifting to *TO* (東) after the consolidation of all Type 14 production at Kokubunji. Although the very early 1934 "D" marked pistols are rare, as are those 1935 specimens marked with the *SHI* character (志), there is little knowledge of or current demand for these variants, and their occurrence is only of interest to advanced collectors.

• **"Kokubunji hybrids":** As noted above, a small number of late Kokura Type 14s were built with receivers and some small parts that were evidently transferred to Kokura from the Kokubunji factory; they have been given the "hybrid" label. After the close of the Kokura production line, remaining parts inventories were transferred to Kokubunji, and were incorporated into Type 14 production there. These pistols, identifiable by internal *HATA* (幡), *KO* (小), or *se* (セ) marks, can also be classified as "hybrids." They are scarce (only two have been identified to date), but it remains to be seen whether they will attract significant collector interest.

• **Standard production variations:** From the "vertical" markings until Kokubunji factory production of the Type 14 ended in August 1944 (*Showa* 19.8), five standard production variations are recognized. The **first variation** includes small trigger guard pistols with horizontal arsenal and factory symbol placement dated from *Showa* 9.2 to 14.9. This variation encompasses an estimated 58,000 pistols. The **second variation** is the large trigger guard transitional, produced from September 1939 until December 1939 (*Showa* 14.9 to 14.12). The large trigger guard was introduced to allow the use of the pistol with heavily gloved hands, and was used on Type 14s produced after the beginning of September 1939 (*Showa* 14.9). This variation includes an estimated 5,850 pistols. (Pistols at both "ends" of this transition, and thus bracketing the two changes involved, are especially sought by collectors, and the overlapping at the points of change adds to this interest.) The **third variation** includes original series pistols having a magazine retainer spring installed in the lower front grip strap, together with a corresponding notch in the lower front of the magazine, added at the beginning of 1940 (*Showa* 15) to prevent accidental magazine loss. At the same time that this change was instituted, the number of grip panel grooves on Kokubunji Type 14s was reduced from 25 to 17. Approximately 27,500 of these pistols were produced before the end of the original serial series was reached in October 1941 (*Showa* 16.10). The **fourth variation** includes an estimated 7,200 pistols in the first serial series produced from October 1941 to June 1942 (*Showa* 16.10-17.6) that have nickeled or blued (starting in *Showa* 16.11) magazines and unblued internal parts. The **fifth variation** includes approximately 13,100 pistols made after May 1942 (*Showa* 17.5) that have hot salt blued parts and blued magazine bodies.

Examples of early (upper, first variation) and later (third variation) Kokubunji factory Type 14s; note differences in trigger guards, grip panel grooving, and the added magazine retainer spring at the lower front of the grip. Second variation pistols are identical to the third variation, except that they lack the magazine retainer spring.

• **Original to first serial series transition:** Some collectors are particularly interested in pistols that closely "bracket" significant changes. As a result, original series pistols with numbers above 99,500 and first series pistols with two- or three-digit serial numbers generally command higher than usual prices.

• **Final production:** By 1944, Kokubunji production of the Type 14 had fallen to very low levels. For this reason, all *Showa* 19-dated examples are scarce. The final three months of production, however, are of particular interest, as examples are notably rarer than "last-ditch" Toriimatsu factory pistols.

• **Production by year:** Kokubunji production of the Type 14 began in December 1933 (*Showa* 8.12), and continued until August 1944 (*Showa* 19.8). Estimated total production numbers by year are:

1933 (*Showa* 8)	**1934** (*Showa* 9)	**1935** (*Showa* 10)	**1936** (*Showa* 11)	**1937** (*Showa* 12)	**1938** (*Showa* 13)
202	1,895	5,709	9,651	17,333	12,428

continued on page 32

1939	**1940**	**1941** (original series)	**1941** (first series)	**1942**
(*Showa* 14)	(*Showa* 15)	(*Showa* 16)	(*Showa* 16)	(*Showa* 17)
17,499	15,245	12,215	4,022	8,562

1943	**1944**
(*Showa* 18)	(*Showa* 19)
5,918	1,798

• **Inspection marking variants**: Unlike Nagoya-Chigusa, Tokyo, and Kokura Type 14s, Kokubunji pistols show little variability in final inspection markings. The Tokyo Arsenal *TO* (東) final inspection mark was used exclusively in the "A" position, except during the March 1935-August 1936 period, which roughly corresponds with the Kokura Arsenal production period, when the *JYO* (條) mark was in exclusive use for final inspections. There is an interesting progression of internal inspection marks that saw the English *N* introduced as a factory mark in 1939, only to be replaced in 1941 by the *kanji SHA* (社, from *Kaisha*, "company"), but pistols with these marks are by no means uncommon.

• **Prototypes and other factory-use pistols:** A very small number of factory cut-away Type 14s were produced by the Kokubunji factory; observed specimens lack factory identification marks, but their origin can generally be determined by other characteristics. Approximately 20 factory prototypes were prepared for the large trigger guard modification; serial nos. 0, 1, 2, 3, 4, 5, 6, 7, 19, 20, and 24 are known. These pistols have 17-groove grip panels, and they have only the factory symbol, or the factory symbol plus the serial number, on the right side. There are also a number of "shop guns" that were apparently assembled at Kokubunji, including single-digit encircled serial number pistols thought to be factory familiarization guns; "dual serial number" pistols with a five digit number above one with four digits, also possibly made for training purposes; and other "experimentals," such as the Kokura receiver used on "shop" gun serial #32207 noted above under "Pure Kukura" Type 14s. Serial numbers on all of these pistols are stamped with dies that have "beaded" points on some digits; this style of numerals was never used for normal Type 14 serial numbers, and they are believed to be diagnostic of "shop" guns.

• **Rare 11-dates:** Kokubunji factory dating in 1936 displays interesting incongruities that have never been well explained. There is a block of "actual" serial numbers (16989-17752) dated *Showa* 11.3, followed by an even smaller block (17793-18140) dated 11.4, and a much larger "second" 11.3 serial block (18236-22218) that evidently contains pistols produced in April through August 1936; no specimens dated *Showa* 11.5 through 11.8 are known. This anomaly undoubtedly was related to the end of Kokura production and the subsequent transfer of remaining parts and tooling to the Kokubunji factory, but the reasoning behind it remains a mystery. Pistols from the "first" 11.3 serial block and those dated 11.4 are rare; only 12 and 6 specimens from each, respectively, are currently known.

Nagoya Arsenal, Toriimatsu factory

• **Pre-production prototypes:** Although full production of the Type 14 at Toriimatsu did not begin until late 1941, a small number of pistols were evidently assembled there in 1939-41 (*Showa* 14-16; four specimens are known). All are built from parts bearing Kokubunji or Kokura inspection marks, although external markings identify them as Nagoya Arsenal products with *Showa* 14 dates. Numerals used for serial numbers and dates are unusually large. Serial numbers are carried forward from assigned Kokubunji and Kokura ranges, and it is believed that these were mechanically defective and incomplete guns that were sent from Kokubunji to Toriimatsu along with new, unmarked receivers to be used in setting up the assembly line, and perhaps in training the workforce, which was to begin production there some eighteen months later.

• **"Double zeros":** The first 185 Type 14s produced by the Toriimatsu factory (serial nos. 50001-50185) are marked with two extra zeros stamped on the right side of the frame immediately above the first two serial digits. The zeros were evidently added after the pistols had received their final surface buffing, as the edges of their impressions are raised, while the edges of the serial digits are flat. The extra zeros signify that the pistols were considered "second class" weapons, not to be issued for regular military service. The reason for this designation is that these pistols were built with experimental non-standard strikers and guides of two different types. One type has an enlarged left-of-center sear lug on the striker, and a corresponding enlarged alignment lug on the guide; the other type

"Double zero" markings on early Toriimatsu factory Type 14 serial number 50036. These markings indicate that the pistol was considered a "second class" weapon, due to non-standard internal parts. *Courtesy Harry L. Derby III.*

Early Toriimatsu factory Type 14 trigger guard with trigger pin end formed into a rounded rivet head (left), and later style with trigger pin end machined flush.

Early Toriimatsu factory Type 14 with standard grooved cocking knob and long rear sight base (left), and later Toriimatsu pistol with modified cylindrical cocking knob and short rear sight base.

has a standard-width centered sear lug on the striker and alignment lug on the guide. Both types have bolt slots cut specifically to fit, and neither will work properly with a standard width left-of-center lug striker and guide. For this reason they could not be repaired by field depots in the event of striker breakage, so they were assigned "second class" status. Most "double-zero" specimens are in excellent condition as a result, but at least two are known to have seen field service. To date, 31 examples of this variant have been reported. Among these, serial #50185 is "double-zero" marked, evidently by mistake, as it has a standard striker, guide, and bolt. Serial #50189 is known not to be marked with extra zeros. One other apparently genuine "Double-Zero" is known from the second serial series; it is serial #50749, and is marked on the left side and on all internal parts with two small zeros. The significance of this marking is unknown. The "Double-Zero" variant is highly prized by collectors; unfortunately, at least one early standard production gun, serial #52626, has been the object of fakery, with artificial "double-zero" markings added. Kokubunji first series serial #15928 is also known to have been marked with fake double zeros. Both pistols also carry fake 16-petal Imperial chrysanthemums, which were never officially applied to Japanese-made pistols.

• **Standard Production variants:** Six standard production variants are recognized. The **first variation** has the ends of the trigger pins exposed and formed into rounded rivet heads, as was done by all other manufacturers of the Type 14. This variant occurs from *Showa* 17.2 to 18.1, with its endpoint very close to the 18.1 to 18.2 transition at about serial #64000; it includes approximately 12,000 pistols. The **second variation** has the outer faces of the trigger pin holes countersunk, and the riveted pin heads are machined flush with the edge of the trigger guard, making the pins nearly invisible. This variant occurs from *Showa* 18.2 to 18.11, and includes approximately 88,000 pistols. The **third variation** begins with the start of the second series in *Showa* 18.11, and continues until the replacement of the grooved cocking knob with the cylindrical type in *Showa* 18.12-19.1. It includes approximately 8,300 pistols. The **fourth variation** occurs in *Showa* 18.12, 19.1, and 19.2, and includes approximately 6,700 pistols with fine-knurled cylindrical cocking knobs, although this number is open to question, due to extensive overlapping that occurs at both ends of its occurrence. This variation also includes the transition from the "long" (17 mm) to "short" (14 mm) rear sight as a result of a minor change in the machining of the receiver bridge, and a change from the original undercut rear sight notch to a simplified square cut notch; at least two transitional sub-variants thus exist, but they are not generally recognized or sought by collectors. The **fifth variation** occurs from *Showa* 19.2 to 19.11, and includes approximately 48,000 pistols with coarse-knurled cylindrical cocking knobs and grooved grip panels. The **sixth variation** occurs from *Showa* 19.11 to 20.6, and includes approximately 8,800 standard production pistols with ungrooved "slab" grips.

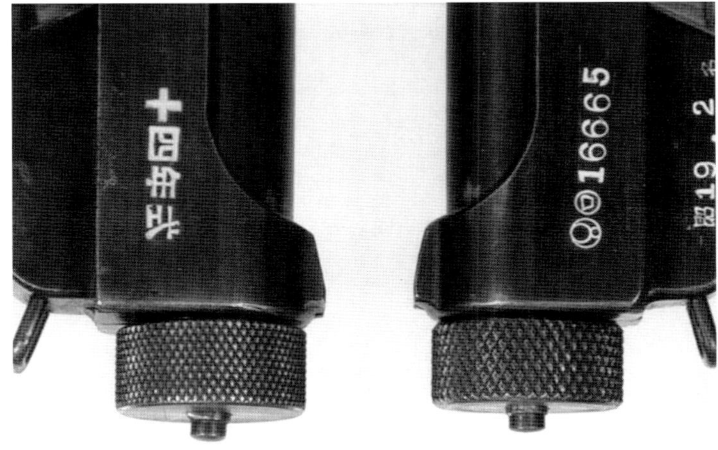

Cylindrical Toriimatsu factory cocking knobs with fine knurling (left) and later coarse knurling. The fine-knurled knob was produced only for a short time because it provided an unsatisfactory gripping surface.

• **Striker variants:** The first standard production pistols after the "double zero" series utilized normal 73 mm strikers and 47 mm guides. Beginning in about *Showa* 17.6, these were replaced by shorter 65 mm strikers and 54 mm guides; this change was evidently planned in advance, as pistols with early 73 mm strikers have bolts cut to accept the shorter model. Late in the first serial series (in the approximate serial range 88000-92000) a second striker modification was introduced that enlarged the tip from its original diameter of 1.5 mm to 2.2 mm, with a corresponding enlarged clearance hole in the bolt. In *Showa* 19.2, the striker tip was reduced slightly to 1.9 mm. The bolt clearance hole was reduced some months later (between *Showa* 19.5 and 19.7), and late production bolts will not accept the "very large tip" strikers.

• **Minor variants:** There are two minor variants that may be of interest to some collectors In *Showa* 19.5, a change was made in grip panel screw threads, and the early "coarse" and later "fine" screws are not interchangeable. The change in screw threads occurred near second series serial #37000. A small number of sixth variation pistols from the 71587-71598 serial range, and from unserialized "last ditch" production, have been reported with chrome-lined barrels.

• **"Last ditch":** Beginning as early as *Showa* 20.5, efforts were underway at the Toriimatsu factory to bolster pistol production by every possible means, even as shortages of materials, supplies, and power, coupled with direct damage from air raids, made this task increasingly difficult. By late *Showa* 20.6 (the highest known "standard production" Type 14 is *Showa* 20.6 serial #71894, while the lowest reported "parts gun" lacking final inspection is serial #70979) formal inspection procedures were suspended, and assembly of pistols from existing stocks of new, cannibalized, and even previously rejected parts was carried out on an emergency basis. An estimated 150 such pistols were assembled in late *Showa* 20.6; 800 in 20.7 (45 examples are known); and 500 in *Showa* 20.8 (four examples are known). Several examples are known of pistols that carry earlier serial numbers and/or dates, and were evidently rejected and shelved earlier in the production process, only to be taken out and re-worked into at least marginally serviceable weapons during the final months of the war. Additionally, more than 1,000 pistols may have been assembled without serial numbers or dates during this period. (All of these estimates rely heavily on guesswork, as there are significant gaps between reported specimens, and it is not known how many receivers may have been assigned serial numbers but were never completed, or how many unserialized guns may have been produced. Much of the evidence that would answer these questions was gathered up and destroyed by U.S. occupation forces after the end of the war.) These "last-ditch" pistols may exhibit any combination of finished, unfinished, numbered, unnumbered, improvised, or incomplete components from any of the five manufacturers. Some also carry markings applied either by U.S. ordnance personnel, or by the GIs who picked them up. To many people they are simply "junk," but to specialized collectors they are particularly interesting, because they portray the final desperate days of the war in Japan. When recognized for what they are, they command premium prices.

• **Production by year**: Estimated Toriimatsu factory production totals by year (excluding pistols not serialized by the factory) are:

1941 (*Showa* 16)	**1942** (*Showa* 17)	**1943** (first series) (*Showa* 18)	**1943** (second series) (*Showa* 18)	**1944** (*Showa* 19)	**1945** (*Showa* 20)
76	11,399	38,524	8,000	58,195	7,105

• **Inspection marks:** All Toriimatsu Type 14s (except for uninspected "last-ditch" pistols) carry the Nagoya Arsenal *NA* (名) "A" position final inspection mark, with *NA* and *ri* (リ) marks, plus the interim inspection mark, on internal parts. Some very late pistols carry "○" marks on the sides of the grip straps. There are no recognized Toriimatsu inspection marking variants.

• **Prototypes and factory-use pistols (special purpose):** One Toriimatsu pressure-test pistol is known. Several pistols are also known that have dual serial numbers—one normally placed five-digit number, and a separate four-digit number placed below and forward of the first—that are thought to have been used for training of factory workers. Some of these appear to have built-in "defects" that workers may have been required to identify and propose remedies. There are also a very limited number of pistols that lack normal right-side markings, and have encircled serial numbers stamped on the butt that were factory-use pistols. One "last-ditch" Type 14 is known with specially marked non-standard internal parts and the *kanji* inscription *Kokoromiru*, "first time trial" scribed on the left side.

Magazines

Type 14s are often found with mismatched magazines, due to a variety of factors that resulted in loss during use, and later restoration with either arsenal re-matched or field substituted replacements. Arsenal re-matched magazines will have old numbers lined through or stamped out in a variety of ways, with new numbers added to serialize them to the newly matched pistol. There are a considerable number of "odd" magazines held by dealers and collectors, and individuals with mismatched guns often search for "proper" substitutes to match and upgrade their specimens. (This effort is often not effective, because "matching numbers" do not necessarily equate to a "proper" matched magazine. With the exception of Nagoya Toriimatsu Type 14s, the magazine inspection mark is almost always the same as that used for the "A" position final inspection on the pistol; Toriimatsu magazines do not always carry the *NA* mark.) The "second," or spare magazine provided with each pistol will be marked like the "first," except that a "dot" is stamped just above the serial number.

Eight variants, or "types" of the Type 14 magazine are recognized, and they are presented as an aid in determining whether or

Early Type 14 holster with exterior features representative of Types I-IV; differences are in the shape and material used in the strap hanger rings, and in the presence or absence of the internal spare striker pouch. *Courtesy Harry L. Derby III.*

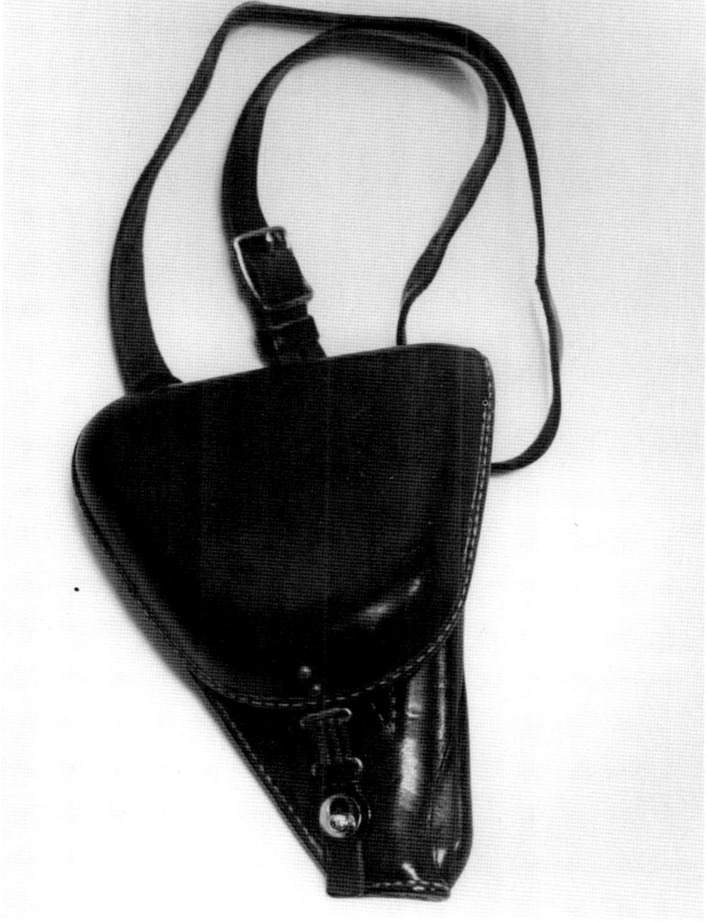

Mid-production Type 14 holster with spring-loaded closure strap and nickel-plated latchplate, Type VI. Type V and VII holsters are similar, except that the former has a brass latchplate, while the latter has a latchplate made of black lacquered steel. Later Type IX and Type X holsters are similar to the Type VII, but have rubberized canvas bodies and clamshells, while the transitional Type VIII has a rubberized canvas body and a leather clamshell. *Courtesy Harry L. Derby III.*

not a magazine is actually correct for a specific pistol. Other differences exist; only those needed for identification are displayed. It should also be noted that the early *Taisho* Era magazines are very rare, but are distinguishable only by their serial numbers; any two-digit Type I is probably a *Taisho*, and three digit Type I magazines numbered below #113 with early inspection marks may be *Taisho*; there is unfortunately no way to be certain of this.

Latch Body Type	Retainer Notch Manufacturer	Base Dates	Spring Finish	Inspection Shape	Material	Notch	Marks
I	Nagoya	*Taisho* 15- *Showa* 7	Nickel	Triangle	Aluminum	No	門 田 筒 □ ⬠ 達 [symbol] [symbol] [symbol] 名 チ
II	Tokyo	" 3-7	Nickel	Square	Aluminum	No	none, 三 吉 [symbol] 大
III	Kokura*	" 7-11	Nickel	Square	Aluminum	No	セ
IV	Kokubunji	" 8-11	Nickel	Square	Aluminum	No	東, ト, 條
V	Kokubunji	" 11-14	Nickel	Square	Alloy	No	東, N
VI	Kokubunji	" 15-17	Nickel	Square	Alloy	Yes	東, N
VII	Kokubunji	" 17-19	Blued	Square	Alloy	Yes	東, 社
VIII	Toriimatsu	" 16-20	Blued	Square	Alloy	Yes	名, リ, ○, [symbol]

*Distinctive flat "ring" around grooves on base

Modern replacement magazines for the Type 14 have also been produced in the U.S. They are blued with an aluminum base, and can easily be identified by the finger recesses on the sides of the base, which are circular, and approximately 4 mm deep, but not grooved, and by the two-piece spot-welded body construction. The base is attached to the body with a single rolled steel pin. The follower and its button are plastic, and is too low in the rear to hold the bolt open when the pistol is empty. The forward edge of the magazine's mouth is lower than on originals, and in some cases this prevents it from activating the magazine safety on the pistol. This magazine will fit and function very satisfactorily on some Type 14s, but not on others. (The same is true of non-matching original magazines.) It functions well when properly fitted, and is a suitable "shooter" accessory in many cases, but holds no historic value for the collector.

Valuation of Type 14s is highly variable because of the wide range in condition, and the large number and differing rarity of variations. Almost any specimen that is complete and free from significant internal corrosion and pitting can be expected to bring $175 to $200 simply as a "parts gun." A specimen with a relatively common manufacturer and production date in very good condition typically will bring $350 to $400, or somewhat less with more exterior wear, a mis-matching magazine, or a minor defect, such as a broken magazine retainer spring. Fine examples of common production pistols will generally bring $100 to $150 more than more average ones, and an accompanying matching second magazine will add $75 to $100 to the value of the pistol alone. The inclusion of other original accessories also adds significantly to the overall value of the pistol, depending on rarity and condition.

Values of the more uncommon variants of the Type 14 are dependent upon individual condition, rarity, and collector appeal. Early Nagoya, Tokyo, and Kokura Arsenal pistols command significantly higher prices than the more common guns from the World War II production years, and transitional variants, such as Kokubunji pistols produced during the period between the adoption of the enlarged trigger guard and the addition of the magazine retainer spring, generate increased collector interest—and value. Rare dates will significantly increase value, and especially desirable variants, such as vertically marked Kokubunji pistols and those from the Taisho-era Nagoya Arsenal production, may command prices ranging from $5,000 to more than $10,000. "Last-ditch" specimens and oddities, such as prototypes and factory cutaway specimens, also require careful evaluation.

Accessories

The Type 14 was issued with its matching second magazine, a holster and strap, a braided cotton lanyard, and a steel cleaning rod. Pistols made after the beginning of 1932 were also issued with a second matching striker, stored in a small pocket located on the front of the holster next to the ammunition pouch. A narrow waist belt was also issued with the Type 14, but it was not always used. Cotton patches sized to fit behind the cartridge boxes in the ammunition pouch were also issued, as were at least two types of plastic or plastic coated fabric holster liners, apparently intended to protect the pistol from moisture and dust. A printed paper manual and a cloth disassembly guide were also available for issue with the Type 14.

There are eleven recognized variants of the standard Type 14 holster. They are:

Type I – Leather, oval brass rings, solid closure strap, no spare striker pouch
Type IA – Identical to Type I, but with added spare striker pouch
Type II – Leather, square brass rings, solid closure strap, no spare striker pouch
Type III – Leather, square brass rings, solid closure strap, spare striker pouch added
Type IV – Leather, square steel rings, solid closure strap, spare striker pouch added
Type V – Leather, square brass rings, spring-loaded closure strap with brass plate
Type VI – Leather, square chromed steel rings, spring-loaded closure strap with chromed steel plate
Type VII – Leather, square lacquered steel rings, spring-loaded closure strap with lacquered steel plate
Type VIII – Rubberized canvas body with leather clamshell
Type IX – Rubberized canvas body and clamshell, with rubberized canvas spare striker pouch
Type X – Rubberized canvas body and clamshell, with leather spare striker pouch (clamshell is slightly narrower than on the Type IX).

A wide variety of non-standard holsters were also used with the Type 14. Shoulder holsters were provided for aircraft and tank crews, and a number of small manufacturers produced custom or substitute holsters for individual purchase. Cut-down versions of standard holsters are also occasionally encountered.

Several reproductions of the Type 14 leather holster have been marketed, in varying degrees of quality and faithfulness to the original design. Some carry replicas of original makers' marks, while others are clearly stamped with the identification of the current manufacturer. In some cases careful examination may be necessary to tell them from originals, especially if they have been artificially "aged." In general, the rivet pattern on the closure strap latchplate will distinguish replica holsters from the originals (see illustration, Chapter V).

Shoulder straps used with Type 14 holsters are made of unwelted cowhide leather 23 mm in width, and generally consist of two segments sewn together, although replacement or non-standard straps are occasionally encountered. Hardware may be of brass, galvanized steel, chrome-plated steel, or black lacquered steel, and generally matches the material used on the holster fittings.

The waist belt issued with the Type 14 was made of cowhide leather until 1943, when rubberized canvas was substituted. Belts are approximately 1 meter (39") long and 20 mm in width, with a wider 35 mm section directly under the buckle and two keepers. Buckles exhibit the same range of materials and finishes used on the shoulder straps. The waist belts are uncommon.

Type 14 lanyards are made of braided cotton cord with a stitched leather slide and keeper. They are usually 6 or 7 mm in diameter; early lanyards are light brown in color, while later ones are light green. Originals are scarce; good quality reproductions are available for more modest prices, and can generally be identified by the use of synthetic fiber.

Cleaning rods for the Type 14 are made of steel; early production pieces are nickel plated, and almost always carry a factory inspection mark. Later production rods are blued, and may or may not show inspection marks; very late "last-ditch" rods are unblued and uninspected, and are rare. Original rods are 163-165 mm in length, with two bends at one end forming a handle and magazine loading tool, and the other end flattened and slotted for a patch, with a blunt tip. At least two different modern reproductions of this tool have been produced; they are blued, and can be readily identified by comparing the forming of the two ends with original rods.

Ammunition for the Type 14 was packaged in 15-round boxes made of tan or brown cardboard, marked in *kanji*:

十四年式拳銃實包
十五發

or

一四年式拳銃實包
十五發

Both read "Fourteen Year Type Handgun Loaded Ammunition / 15 Rounds," although the character used for the first digit in the type designation is "ten" in the more common labeling on the left, and "one" in the labeling on the right. As issued, these boxes were bound together in pairs with string to fit the standard holster's ammunition pouch. Original boxes of cartridges are very desirable for completing an assemblage of pistol and accessories. Separate leather pouches for carrying single or (much more rarely) double cartridge boxes were also issued by the Japanese. These are less commonly associated with the Type 14 than with the Type 94, which had no ammunition pouch built into its holster.

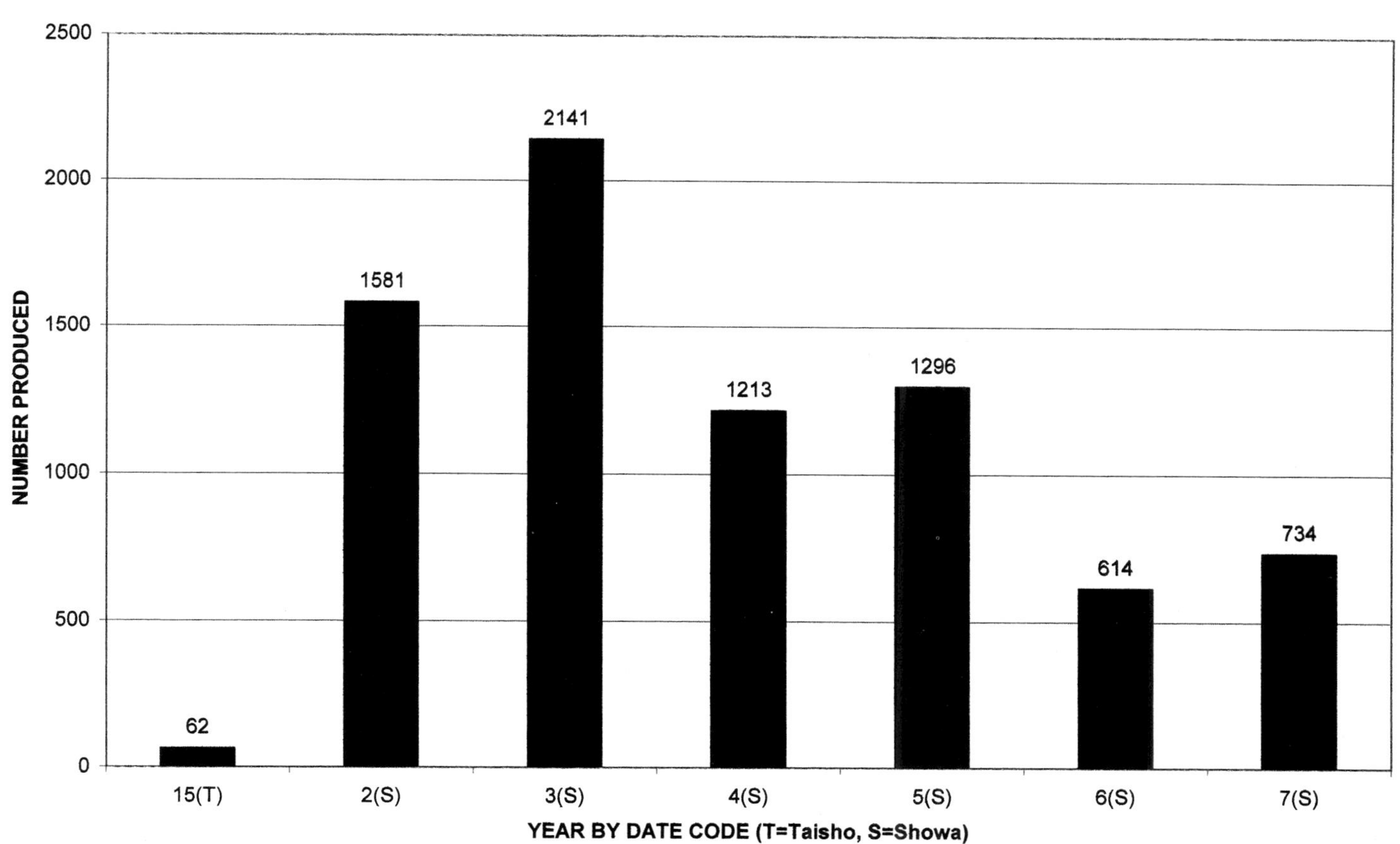

KNOWN TYPE 14 PRODUCTION, TOKYO AND KOKURA ARSENALS

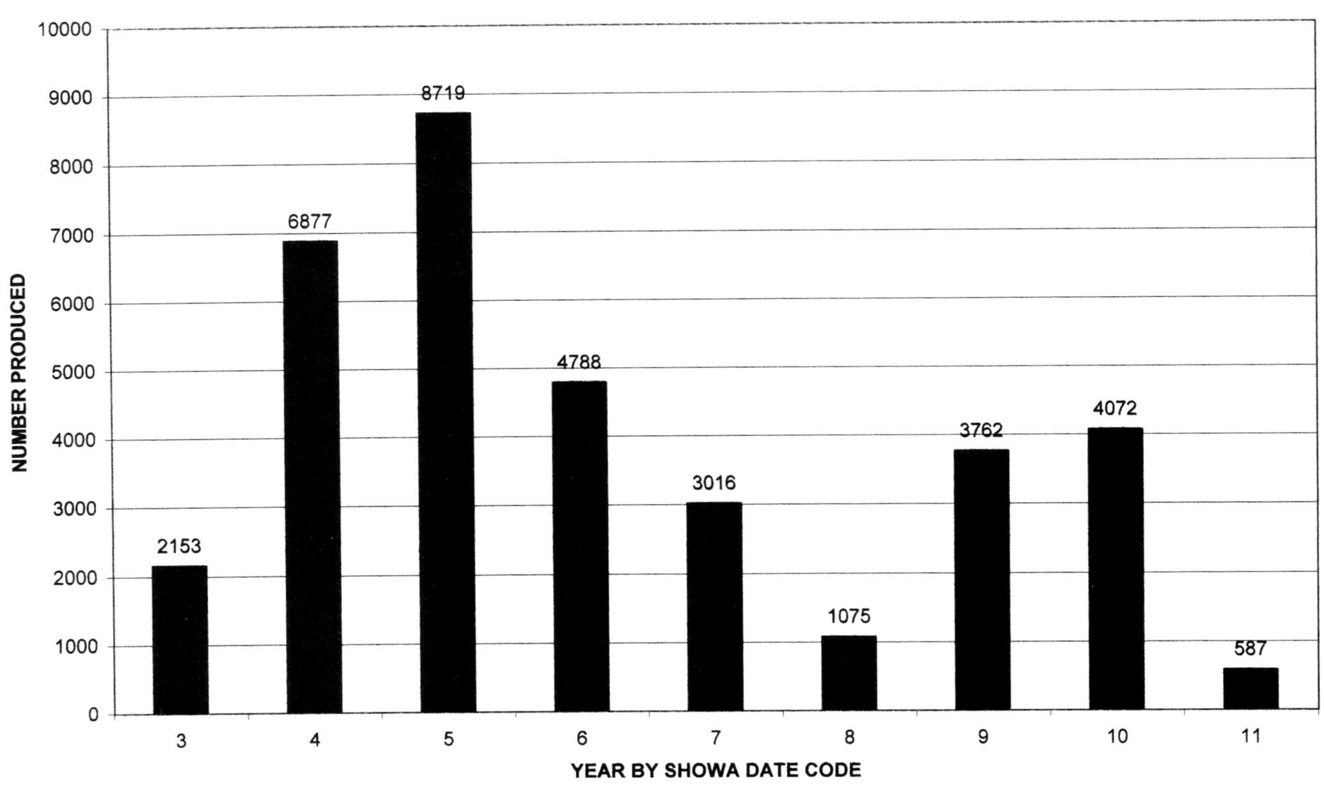

KNOWN TYPE 14 PRODUCTION, NAMBU KOKUBUNJI FACTORY

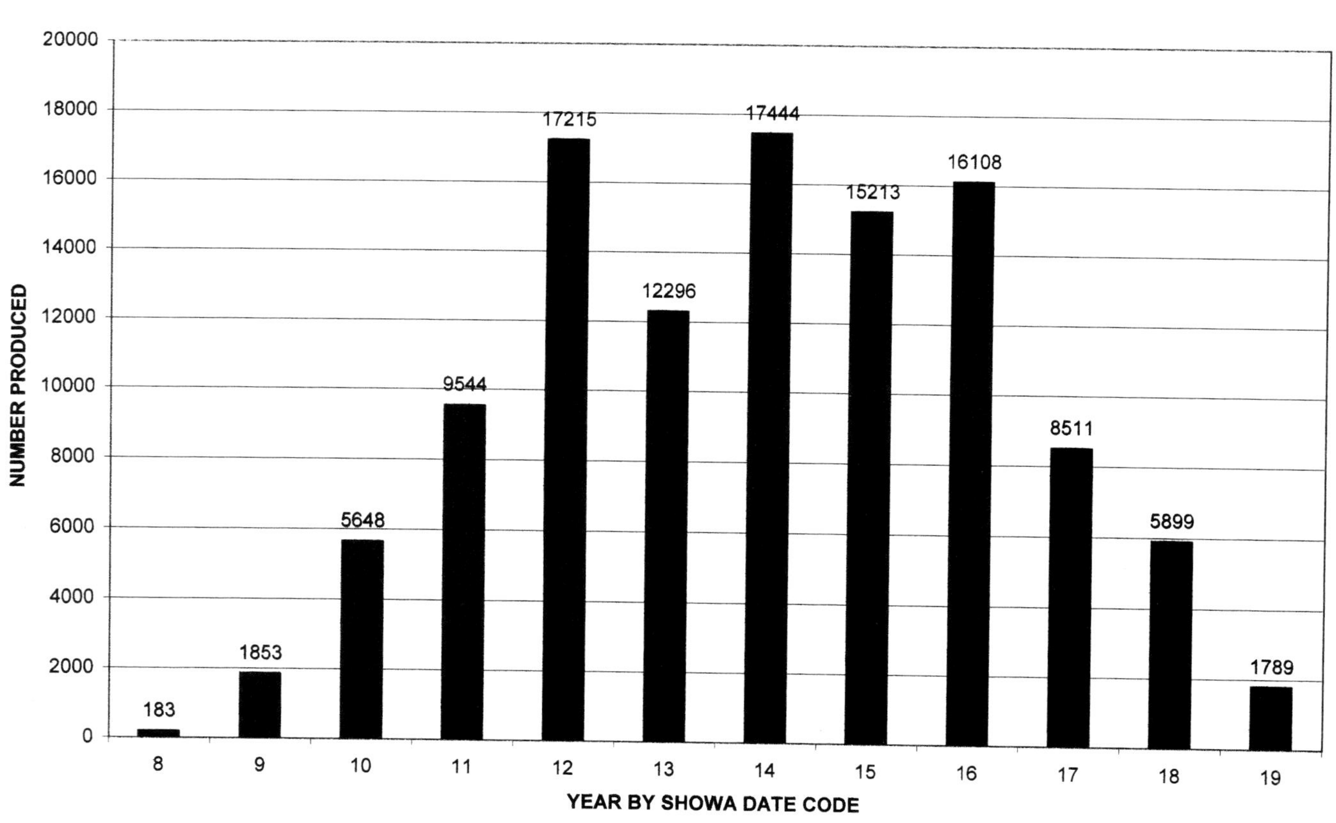

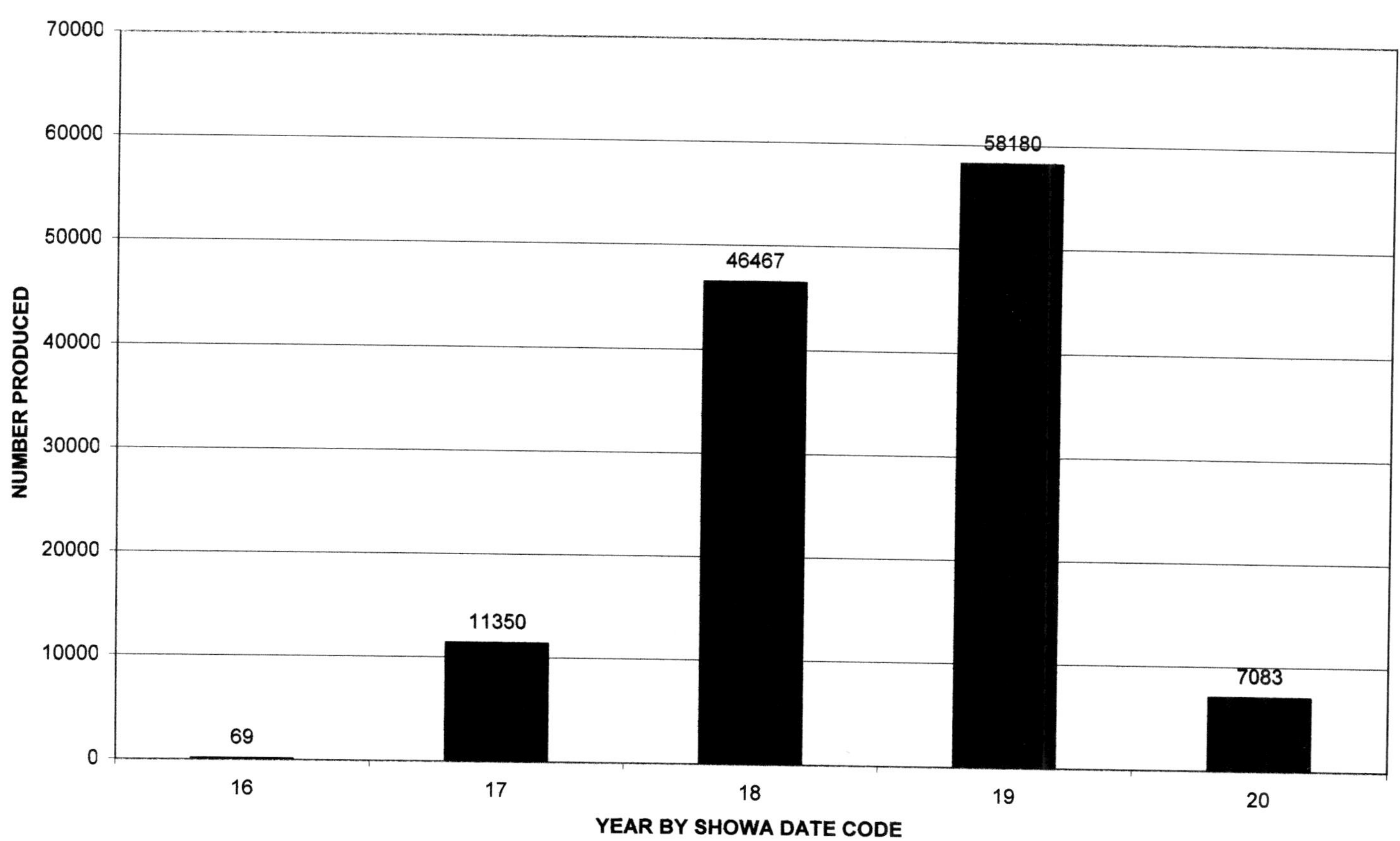
KNOWN TYPE 14 PRODUCTION, NAGOYA-TORIIMATSU FACTORY
70000
60000
50000
40000
30000
20000
10000
0
NUMBER PRODUCED
69
11350
46467
58180
7083
16
17
18
19
20
YEAR BY SHOWA DATE CODE

VIII

The Type 94

The Type 94 was developed in response to demand by the Imperial Japanese Army for a small handgun in the standard 8 mm caliber that could be mass produced. It was designed by Kijiro Nambu after his retirement from the Army, and was adopted in 1934 (Japanese calendar year 2594, from which the type designation is derived). Production began at Nambu's Kokubunji factory in 1935 (*Showa* 10), and continued until June 1945 (*Showa* 20.6). Total production came to approximately 71,100 pistols (the highest known example is #71084).

Like the Type 14, Type 94 pistols carry their year and month of manufacture stamped on the rear of the right side of the receiver. These dates add significantly to the historical study of the pistol's development and production; they also add considerably to the number of variants of interest to collectors. Also like the Type 14, overlapping of changes and out-of-sequence dates are relatively common. However, Type 94 production also includes a significant block of "off-date" pistols that constitute an important variant.

The type 94 has been the target of a great deal of criticism. Some of this is deserved, but much of it is the transparently ignorant repetition of old prejudices. Unlike the family of earlier Nambu designs that began with the 1902 "Grandpa" and culminated in the Type 14, the Type 94 is mechanically unique in virtually all of its features; it is completely Japanese, and completely Nambu. Its primary weaknesses are the result of a lack of Japanese experience in the tactical use of handguns in the combat environment that developed in World War II, and the inability of their arms industry to make major developmental changes in the design once the war reached a climax.

Early (upper, November 1936 serial number 1539) and late (May 1945 serial number 70723) production examples of the Type 94.

An interesting feature of Type 94s is the progression of exterior finishing treatments that were applied through the pistol's production history. Early guns exhibit fine high-polish rust blueing and heat strawing that is the equivalent of the best European military arms of the period. By early 1939 (*Showa* 14) attention to surface polishing began to wane, and by late 1941 (*Showa* 16) it had been abandoned altogether. The year 1942 (*Showa* 17) witnessed the abandonment of nickeling of magazines, and a change from rust blueing to a hot salt bath process. Exterior surface machining standards deteriorated further during 1943 and 1944 (*Showa* 18-19), and the consistency of blueing salts also declined during this period. Even the workmanship evident in type, date, and serial markings declined to the point that these were often misaligned, and applied with as many as three different numeral sizes. During all of this time, internal machining tolerances were held to surprisingly high standards. Exterior quality reached its lowest point near the end of 1944 (*Showa* 19), but it improved markedly by the end of January 1945 (*Showa* 20.1), evidently as a result of a change in supervisory arsenal administration. It was maintained at this level until the end of standard production in June 1945 (*Showa* 20.6), when "last-ditch" assembly efforts produced a relatively small number of guns that were mere specters of their 1935 predecessors. The desperation reflected in this final group of Type 94s makes them especially prized by some advanced collectors.

Identification

The Type 94 is an 8 mm semiautomatic pistol with a 96 mm (3.78") barrel enclosed by a slide. It has fixed sights, a separate bolt with a vertically grooved cocking piece fixed to the rear of the slide by a horizontal crossbolt, an internal hammer, and a six-shot magazine housed in the grip frame. The trigger guard has an unusual forward-jutting oval shape, and is integral with the receiver. The grip frame is short and somewhat small; grip panels are made of either checkered black bakelite or smooth wood. A safety lever is mounted on the left rear of the receiver where it blocks movement of an external sear bar, and a button-type magazine catch is located at the lower left corner of the trigger guard. The pistol is 187 mm (7.36") long and weighs 1 lb 11 oz.

Field Disassembly

Clear the pistol by drawing the cocking knob all the way to the rear, locking the slide against the magazine follower. Inspect the magazine and chamber to ensure that they are unloaded.

Insert a finger into the recess in the bottom of the bolt and push the firing pin all the way forward. While holding it in this position, use a non-marring tool to push the slide crossbolt approximately ¼" to the left. (CAUTION: do not push the crossbolt all the way out of the slide at this time.)

Position the pistol in the left hand, with the thumb through the trigger guard and the fingers over the top of the slide, gripping it firmly to prevent the slide from springing forward when released from the bolt. With the right hand, grasp the protruding end of the crossbolt and pull it out of the slide to the left. Draw the bolt to the rear out of the slide, then allow the slide to move forward slowly under pressure from the recoil spring. If the slide stops when it reaches its battery (forward) position, press in on the front of the barrel; this will unlock the slide and allow it to be removed forward off of the receiver.

Remove the locking block. Withdraw the barrel, recoil spring, and recoil spring guide from the rear of the slide. Remove the firing pin and its spring from the bottom of the bolt. (On late production pistols, the extractor is only "laid in" on the top of the bolt, and may be lifted directly from its recess.) Push in on the magazine catch and remove the magazine from the receiver. If desired, remove the grip panel screws and lift the grip panels off of the receiver.

In reassembling the pistol, do not replace the magazine until the other procedures are completed. After replacing the barrel, recoil spring, and recoil spring guide in the slide, turn it upside-down, and insert the locking block between the two bottom lugs of the barrel. "Start" the slide onto the receiver upside-down, positioning the two spring retaining fingers on the receiver between the recoil spring guide and the front of the chamber. Pull the slide to the rear just far enough so that the crossbolt can be inserted part way into its recess behind the receiver bridge, temporarily restraining the slide.

Reassemble the bolt. Grip the pistol firmly with the left hand as described above for disassembly. With the right hand, push the front of the slide to the rear as far as it will go, remove the crossbolt, insert the bolt assembly into the rear of the slide, and insert the crossbolt ¼" into its recess from the left side of the slide. Insert the right index finger into the bottom of the bolt, push the firing pin all the way forward, and use the right thumb to finish seating the crossbolt. The slide can then be allowed to move forward into battery, and the magazine can be replaced.

Markings

The left side of the pistol bears type *kanji* 式四九, reading from right to left "94 Type." (Very early pistols have the order of the *kanji* reversed, and read from left to right.) Safety position *kanji* are stamped just outside the safety lever's arc of movement. The right side of the receiver carries the Nagoya Arsenal and Kokubunji factory symbols, the *Showa* Era year and month of manufacture preceded by the *SHO kanji* (昭), the serial number, and the supervisory arsenal inspection mark. Location and relative order of these markings changed during production, and they are an interesting source of variations. Factory and interim inspection marks appear on the exterior of the pistol, as well as on internal parts.

Overlapping and out-of-sequence dates

As with the Type 14, the manufacturing process used with the Type 94 involved the use of bins for accumulating and holding parts awaiting assembly. This practice resulted in the "overlapping" of changes when newly made parts incorporating the changes were used to assemble pistols before the stock of "old" parts was completely exhausted. In addition, pistols that had been serialized were apparently removed from the production line, either for additional inspection, or to correct minor imperfections, and were not returned to the line for final inspection, and dating until one or more months later, creating serial numbers that are out of sequence with their dates. This process became increasingly common in the final six to eight months of production, but out-of-sequence examples should not be confused with the distinct block of pistols listed below as "Off-Dates."

Variations

Type 94 variants are categorized on the basis of frame markings, machining changes, dating, magazine design, grip panel design, and other characteristics. Because some of these changes are concurrent, while others were phased in or overlap each other, delineating all of the resulting variations in a single chronological chain is simply not practical. In addition, there are a small number of prototypes and factory use pistols that differ from standard production.

Frame markings: Five frame marking variations are recognized. The differences involve the size, style, and placement of the primary markings, and the order of the arsenal and factory symbols, which was changed twice. The **first variation** includes only a very small number (less than 10) of early pistols dated *Showa* 10.6, and has the arsenal and factory symbols placed close together adjacent to the serial number, while the left side type *kanji* are larger and more delicate in style than on later pistols. (There is some overlapping of *kanji* characteristics between Type 1 and early Type 2 specimens.) The **second variation** has the arsenal and factory symbols widely separated, and uses smaller left side type *kanji*. This variation includes approximately 7,300 pistols produced through mid-*Showa* 14.1, with overlapping in the 7300-7400 serial range. The **third variation** has the arsenal and factory symbols placed close together toward the rear of the receiver, with the order reversed so that Nambu (the stylized character *NAN*) precedes the Nagoya symbol. Left side type *kanji* have also been moved forward from the area over the center of the grip to the rear of the trigger guard. This variant includes approximately 11,800 pistols dated from *Showa* 14.1 to 16.8. The **fourth variation** again reverses the arsenal and factory symbol order so that Nagoya precedes Nambu. This variant includes approximately 22,000 pistols dated from *Showa* 16.8 to approximately 19.1 (the transition from the

First Type 94 marking variation, right side (June 1935 serial number 1). Note also the split-pin frame pivots, unique to very early production.

First Type 94 marking variation (serial number 1), left side.

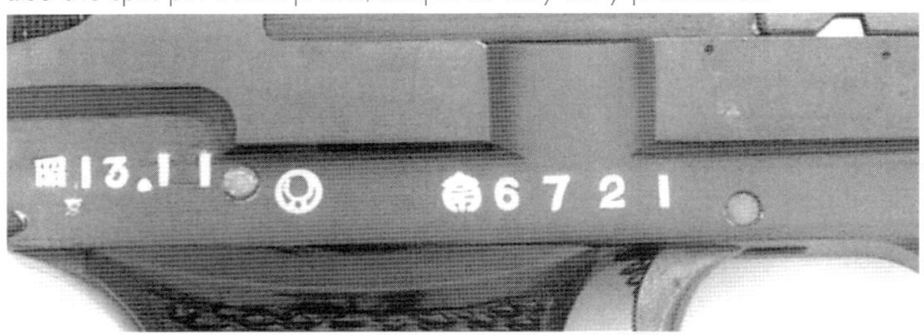

Second Type 94 marking variation (November 1938 serial number 6721), right side.

Second Type 94 marking variation (serial number 6721), left side.

Third Type 94 marking variation (April 1939 serial number 8271), right side.

Third and fourth Type 94 marking variations (serial number 8271), left side.

Fourth Type 94 marking variation (May 1943 serial number 37894), right side.

Fifth Type 94 marking variation (October 1944 serial number 62501), right side.

Fifth Type 94 marking variation (serial number 62501), left side.

fourth to fifth variation is not well established). The **fifth variation** separates the arsenal and factory symbols slightly (approximately 5 mm). It includes approximately 30,000 pistols dated from approximately *Showa* 19.1 through 20.6.

Machining changes: The number of machining changes incorporated in the Type 94 design during its ten-year production history makes up a laundry list of variants that is quite amazing. Fifteen notable design changes have been recorded, producing 25 production variants, plus three transitional ones. (This does not include three recently identified changes in the machining of the rear barrel lug, which interacts with the disconnector during cycling. Detailed descriptions of these relatively minor modifications are beyond the scope of this text, and would be of little value without illustrations.) Many of these occur concurrently with other changes, and not all of the resulting variants have gained collector attention, but all add interest to the position of individual pistols in the overall production history of the type.

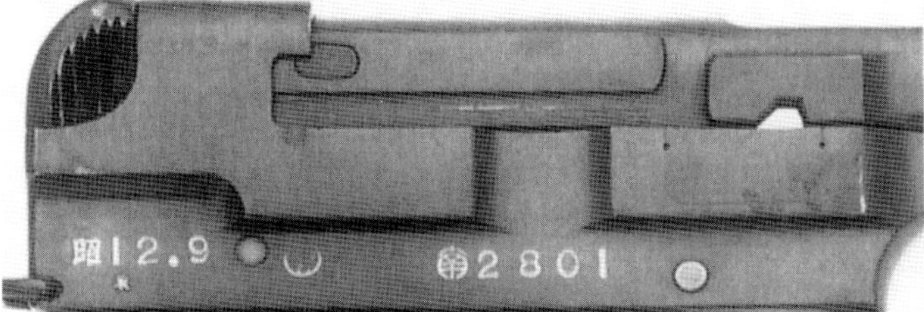

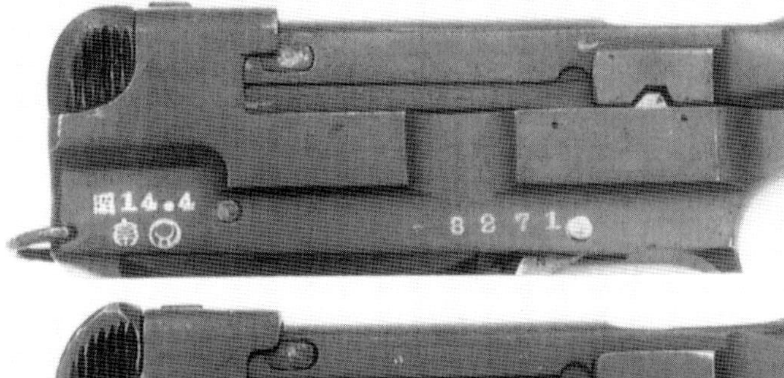

(Top to bottom) Type 94 slide rib variations 1 through 5. Note that the only difference between variations 4 and 5 is a 1 mm vertical reduction in rib width.

• *Frame pivots*: Three variations are recognized. A very small number of early pistols (probably no more than 20) utilize flanged split pins for hammer and trigger pivots. By serial #29, these had been replaced by slotted screws with exposed heads. Beginning in November 1937 (*Showa* 12.11 serial #3792), screw heads were recessed to fit flush with the receiver surface. In addition, one late production specimen, *Showa* 19.2 serial #48451, has original frame screws that have Phillips type heads, rather than the ordinary slotted type. It is not known whether this was a factory prototype or trial pistol, or perhaps a later alteration.

• *Slide ribs*: Five variations are known. Variation 1 ribs are 5 mm wide and 48 mm long, with a 10 mm gap between the front end of the rib and the locking block blister; this variation is limited to approximately the first 50 pistols produced (highest observed specimen is serial #38). Variation 2 ribs are 7.5 mm wide and 52.5 mm long, with a 5.5 mm gap between the rib and the locking block blister; the forward end of the rib is rounded. This variation includes approximately 4,250 pistols made from *Showa* 10.6-12.12, the highest reported specimen being serial #4287. Variation 3 ribs are 8 mm wide and 52.5 mm long, with a 5.5 mm gap between the rib and the locking block blister; the forward end of the rib is square. This variation includes approximately 2,700 pistols, the serial range of reported specimens being 4397-6832. Variation 4 ribs are 8 mm wide and 58 mm long, with no gap between the forward end of the rib and the locking block blister, although a semicircular notch in the lower edge of the rib remains at this point. This varia-

Early (left) and later machining of the forward receiver and slide contours.

Early style sear bar and frame machining above rear of safety lever.

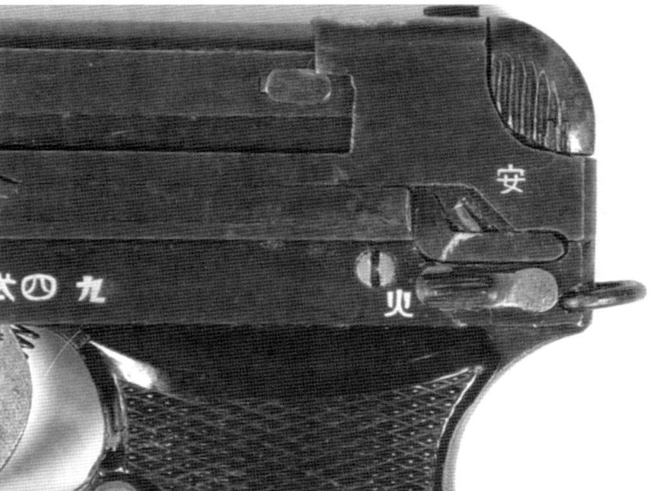

Late style sear bar and frame machining above rear of safety lever.

tion includes approximately 53,000 pistols produced from *Showa* 14.1-19.9. Variation 5 ribs are 7 mm wide and 58 mm long, with a connection to the locking block blister identical to Variation 4. This variation includes approximately 11,000 pistols produced from 19.10-20.6.

• *Bolt*: Two variations are known. The original design included a lower front lug on each side of the magazine clearance slots to ensure proper cartridge alignment during feeding. At the beginning of 1939 (*Showa* 14) these lugs were eliminated to simplify machining.

• *Sear bar and front slide/frame configuration*: This group encompasses two machining changes that were implemented about four months apart, creating three variants: "early," "transitional," and "late." Early pistols have a raised step at the rear of the sear bar, with the receiver completely enclosing the sides of this raised step; the lower forward area of the slide that adjoins the front frame extension is rounded, and the frame extension is 15 mm wide. The transitional variant has the step at the rear of the sear bar eliminated, and the adjacent receiver area below the sear bar machined to match the new flat sear bar contour, while the area above it remains unchanged; the slide and front frame extension remain unchanged. The late variation has the sear bar and surrounding receiver changes of the transitional, while the lower forward slide area is no longer rounded, and the front frame extension has been enlarged to a width of 18 mm. The early variation includes approximately 9,500 pistols dated *Showa* 10.6-14.12; the transitional variant includes approximately 2,700 pistols dated *Showa* 15.1-15.4 (observed serial range 9620-11358); the late variation includes approximately 59,700 pistols dated *Showa* 15.4-20.6.

• *Cocking knob*: Two variations are recognized: the original rounded contour, and the "square-back" introduced in late December 1944 (the earliest known example is *Showa* 20.1 serial #66386), and implemented primarily in January 1945 (*Showa* 20.1) with an overlap of approximately 3,000 pistols. "Late round-back" specimens appear occasionally throughout the rest of Type 94 production.

• *Hammer*: Two variations are known. The original design utilized a sear bar recess cut into the hammer from the bottom (in the cocked position) that engaged the rear of the sear bar at an angle approximately 20 degrees from the vertical, semi-tangential to the hammer's arc of movement. In January 1945 (*Showa* 20.1) the recess was changed to a larger simplified opening cut into the hammer from the rear (in the cocked position) that engaged the bottom of the sear bar horizontally. The shape of the rear of the sear bar was also modified slightly to accommodate this change.

• *Rear sight*: Two variations are known. The original design is "U" shaped as seen from above, with the top of the "U" facing forward. In December 1944 (*Showa* 19.12, beginning between serial nos.

Early (left) and late production specimens showing changes introduced in late 1944 and early 1945. Note rounded vs. square cocking knob, long vs. short rear sight, and checkered bakelite vs. smooth wood "slab" grip panels.

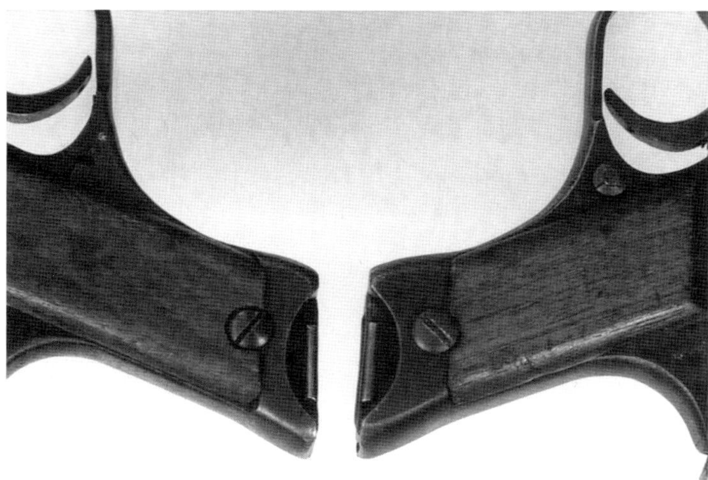

Long (left) and short "slab" grip panels, the latter produced by a simplification in the machining of the lower grip frame introduced in may 1945. The short grip panel variant is found scattered through *Showa* 20.5 and 20.6 specimens at about the same frequency as the standard long grip panel. Short grip panel variants are occasionally found with modified checkered bakelite panels.

65356 and 65860) this was changed to a simple notched crossbar running perpendicular to the long axis of the slide.

• *Side plates*: Two variations are known. The original design utilized sideplates approximately 10 mm in height, fitted into round-bottomed dovetailed recesses machined into the upper portion of the frame. Beginning in January 1945 (*Showa* 20.1) and fully implemented by March, the dovetailed recesses were machined all the way through the frame from top to bottom, resulting in a slightly longer sideplate with a flat bottom, and reducing the machining and fitting time. A transitional variant has been observed that has the left sideplate round-bottomed and the right sideplate square; *Showa* 20.1 serial #66667 and 20.2 serial #68306 are examples.

• *Extractor fitting*: Two variations are recognized. All early Type 94s have hand fitted extractors mounted in dovetailed slots in the top of the bolt; by March 1945 (*Showa* 20.3) the bolt slots were left rectangular, and the extractors were simply "laid in," being retained only by the contact with the inside of the slide preventing the retaining lug from rising out of the bolt recess.

• *Grip frame*: Two variations are known. The original configuration remained standard through April 1945 (*Showa* 20.4), but beginning by May (the earliest reported example is *Showa* 20.3 serial #69391) the machining around the grip screws was simplified, resulting in a shorter recess for the grip panels. The change was never fully implemented before production ended, but "short grip panel" variants are fairly evenly distributed among *Showa* 20.5 and 20.6 dated pistols, and are sought by collectors.

• *Minor variations*: In 1942 (*Showa* 17) a number of pistols were produced that have unusually thick (measured front to rear) triggers, with dimensions as large as 8 mm, as compared to the normal thickness of 4.5-5.5 mm. Specimens from 1942 also usually show finely scribed vertical lines on the surface of the locking block blisters of the slide, corresponding to the four corners of the locking block notch; the significance of these marks is unclear. Some pistols produced in 1944 have unusually thick trigger guards. A small number of late production pistols have four-digit serialized magazines, rather than the usual three digits; there is insufficient data at this time to classify this as a distinct variant, but these "four-digit" pistols often have the thick trigger guards noted above, and have significant date anomalies. While these variants are of interest to some collectors, they are not currently considered significant enough to affect value.

Exterior finish: Early production pistols were rust blued, with their triggers and safeties heat strawed, and interior surfaces left "in the white." Beginning in early 1942 (*Showa* 17.1), the blueing process was changed to a hot salts bath method, leaving all surfaces of treated parts colored; triggers and safeties continued to be heat strawed, and barrels, recoil spring bushings, and firing pins remained unblued. In late 1943 (*Showa* 18) heat strawing was discontinued; barrels, recoil spring bushings, and firing pins remained unblued. In addition, after early 1942 exterior machining and finishing standards were allowed to gradually decline to a degree that is sometimes downright shocking in its crudeness. Exterior quality reached its lowest ebb in late 1944 (*Showa* 19), but improved markedly during January 1945, and was held to moderately good standards until the end of production. Some collectors are especially interested in crude late-war examples. It should be noted, however, that the exterior condition of these pistols does not generally reflect the quality of internal machining and fitting.

Magazine types: Four types are recognized: Type 1, nickeled with flat base plate; Type 2, nickeled with ribbed base plate; Type 3, blued with rectangular serrated follower button; and Type 4, blued with round checkered follower button. The change from Type 1 to Type 2 occurred in *Showa* 12.7; the change from Type 2 to type 3 occurred in *Showa* 17.1; and the change from Type 3 to Type 4 occurred in *Showa* 19.8.

Grip panel types: Four types are recognized: Type 1 is made of black bakelite, with a fine checkered pattern and an upper brass retainer plate pinned in place (except for a few very early specimens); Type 2 is made of black bakelite with a coarse checkering pattern and an upper brass retainer plate pinned in place; Type 3 is made of black bakelite with a medium checkered pattern and an upper brass retainer plate molded in place; and Type 4 is made of smooth wood (often referred to as a "slab grip") with no retainer plate, a change introduced in July 1944 (*Showa* 19.7) because of a shortage of bakelite resin. A sub-variant of the Type 4 is the short grip frame panel, which is usually made of wood, although improvised cut-down panels made of bakelite are occasionally observed.

"Off-dates": During 1942 (*Showa* 17) a group of parts for approximately 2,500 pistols was withdrawn from the inventory at Kokubunji, and was sent to the Niikura factory for fitting and assembly, reportedly because the Niikura factory had been idled while awaiting production decisions by the Japanese Ordnance Board on other weapons. The receivers for these pistols had been serialized, but not dated. The following year the completed pistols were returned to the Kokubunji factory, where they were inspected, dated, and finished. Because of the delay, pistols with serial numbers from the 26,000-29,000 range that would be expected to carry dates of *Showa* 17.6 are instead dated *Showa* 18.6, 18.7, and 18.8. The reason for the dating irregularity has been the subject of much discussion, and "off-date" Type 94s are of considerable interest to collectors. Approximately 115 "off-date" specimens have been reported from the serial range 26047-28482, with overlapping at both ends; of this group, pistols dated *Showa* 18.8 are least common. However, it should be noted that "correct" pistols dated *Showa* 18.6, 18.7, and 18.8 are considerably rarer than the "off-dates" themselves.

Inspection marks: Unlike the Type 14, the inspection marks found on Type 94 pistols follow a logical and consistent progression with no surprises. They are, for the most part, the same marks used on Kokubunji Type 14 pistols from 1935 through 1944 (*Showa* 10 – 19), with some changes after the end of Kokubunji Type 14 production. The *JYO* (條) final inspection mark was used from June 1935 through August 1936 (*Showa* 10.6 – 11.8). The standard Tokyo Arsenal final inspection mark *TO* (東) was used from September 1936 through December 1944 (*Showa* 11.9 – 19.12). In January 1945 (*Showa* 20.1), inspection responsibility for the Type 94 was passed to the Nagoya Arsenal, and the inspection mark *NA* (名) was used from that point until the end of production. However, some late *Showa* 20.5 pistols, and many of those dated 20.6, do not carry final inspection marks; by the time they were received by Nagoya Arsenal the inspection process had been discontinued. During that period, the *NAN* (南) mark was applied to the left side of the frame as a factory inspection mark. Other factory marks used are the English letter *N* (1939-41, *Showa* 14-16), the *kanji* *SHA* (社) 1941-44 (*Showa* 16-19), and the interim inspection mark

.

Annual production totals: Estimates of Type 94 production by year are:

1935	**1936**	**1937**	**1938**	**1939**	**1940**
(*Showa* 10)	(*Showa* 11)	(*Showa* 12)	(*Showa* 13)	(*Showa* 14)	(*Showa* 15)
701	995	2,688	2,713	2,511	5,916
1941	**1942**	**1943** standard	**1943** off-dates	**1944**	**1945**
(*Showa* 16)	(*Showa* 17)	(*Showa* 18)	(*Showa* 18)	(*Showa* 19)	(*Showa* 20)
7,151	7,620	12,777	2,973	20,150	4,855

"Last-Ditch": Like the Type 14, the Type 94 went through a period of final desperate assembly near the end of the war, resulting in a group of unfinished, unserialized, incomplete, and improvised pistols. Unlike the Type 14, however, the end of Type 94 production was apparently a planned process that ended in June 1945 (*Showa* 20.6), after which all Kokubunji pistol production machinery was moved to the Nagoya Toriimatsu factory, where it was found at the end of the war. As a result, "last-ditch" Type 94s are considerably rarer than such specimens of the Type 14; no pistols dated after *Showa* 20.6 are known, and only five undated specimens have been reported. These pistols are of great interest to specialized collectors.

Prototypes and factory-use pistols

A prototype from which the Type 94 was later developed was patented by Kijiro Nambu in November 1929, and was probably produced in 1930-31, including at least six different pistols of at least two slightly different configurations. One specimen (serial no 6) is in a private U.S. collection, and it is believed that at least one other example (serial #2) was brought home by a GI returning from the Pacific, although it has not been located. These pistols are of great interest to advanced collectors.

In addition, several "production prototypes" and factory-use pistols have been identified. These pistols are of standard design, but have either had the right-side markings removed, or have had these markings only partially applied. Two such pistols, serial numbers 7 and 8, were modified from 1938 production guns, and were probably used for worker familiarization and training. A third, also evidently produced in 1938, carries no external serial number, but is numbered 1 on the bottom of the cocking knob. This pistol is the only authenticated factory cut-away Type 94, and has mechanism viewing cuts on its rear and left side. A fourth pistol, serial #20621, carries no date, and no evidence of the date having been removed; the left grip panel carries painted *kanji* that are no longer legible due to wear, but this is also believed to be a factory-use pistol. Two other identical specimens, unserialized and carrying only the right

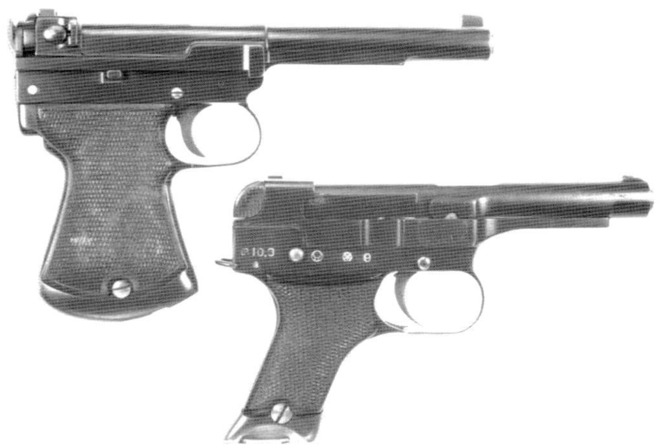

Prototype Type 94 serial number 6 (above) and early standard production Type 94, June 1935 serial number 9. *Robert E. Hogan Collection, photo by Scott T. Hogan.*

side date "19," have the "square-back" cocking knob introduced in *Showa* 20.1, and are believed to be factory prototypes for this modification.

Valuation of the Type 94, like the Type 14, is highly variable. In general, current Type 94 values are not commensurate with their scarcity—they commonly sell for prices that are roughly equivalent to those of the Type 14, even though approximately four times as many Type 14s were produced as Type 94s. Specimens from the more common production years in very good condition typically sell for $400 to $500, with fine specimens bringing additional premiums of $50 to $100. Very early specimens (especially those with *Showa* 10 dates) in fine condition will bring prices of $2,000 to $2,500, and early intermediate examples (*Showa* 11 through 13) also carry additional value, depending on date and condition. Uncommon variants, such as "Off-dates" and transitional examples, typically bring prices that are $50 to $150 above the more common production guns; specimens from the last month of production (*Showa* 20.6), and examples of "Last-ditch" production also generate increased collector interest, and thus higher prices. The inclusion of the matching second magazine will add $75 to $100 to the value of the pistol alone, and the inclusion of original accessories may also add significantly to the value of the "package."

Accessories

The Type 94 was issued with its matching second magazine, a holster and shoulder strap, and a steel cleaning rod. (No waist belt was

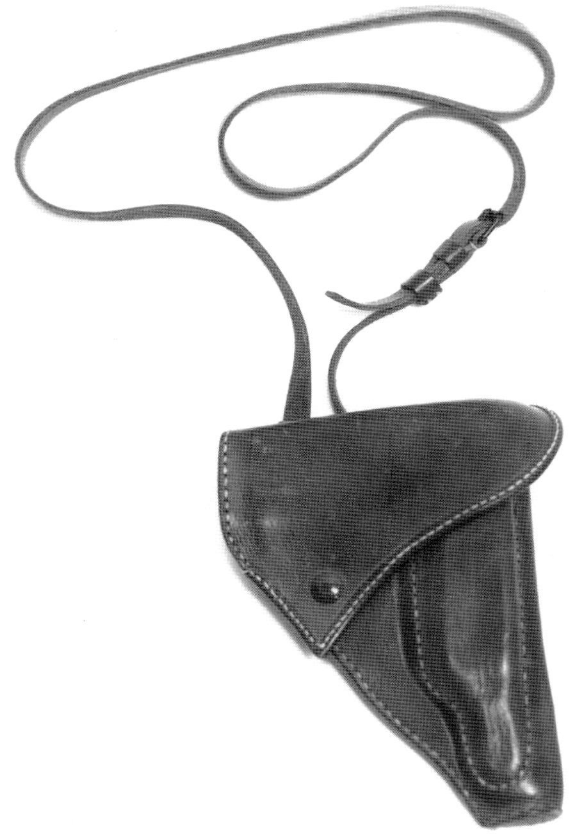

Standard leather Type 94 holster and strap. *Courtesy Harry L. Derby III.*

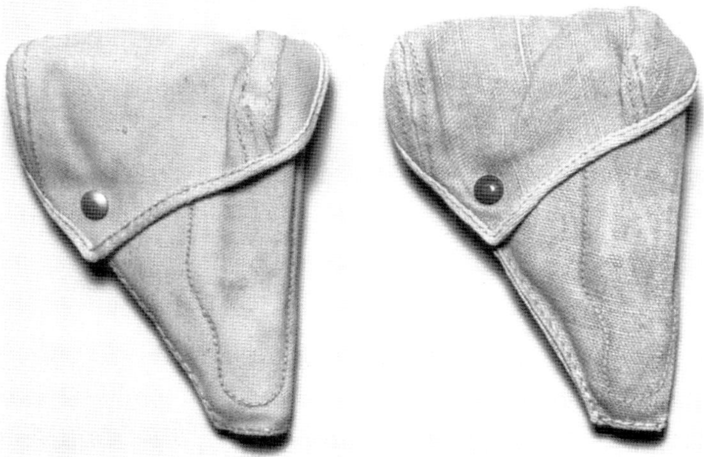

Late production canvas Type 94 holsters: fine-weave variant (left) and coarse-weave variant. *Buck Squires Collection, photo by Terrell Hoffman.*

issued with the Type 94.) Spare ammunition pouches containing one or two standard 15-round boxes of 8 mm cartridges are sometimes found attached to Type 94 straps, but they were apparently issued separately. A printed instruction booklet was also prepared for the Type 94, but it is rare, and whether it was commonly issued with the pistols is not known. A woven canvas belt with a sliding metal loop fastener is sometimes found with late-issue pistols. Surprisingly, lanyards appear not to have been regularly issued with the Type 94. Although individual pistols are sometimes found equipped with the standard Type 14 lanyard, more commonly Type 94s are found with improvised lanyards made from parachute cord or similar material.

Standard Type 94 holsters are of four major types: cowhide leather, pigskin leather, coarse-weave canvas, and fine-weave canvas; both canvas variants have leather belt loops and strap attachment tabs. Another rare canvas variant has been identified with slightly larger dimensions, but it is thought to have been designed for the Type 2 Hamada. All of these types have metal snap closures, and were originally accompanied by leather shoulder straps 13 mm wide, with the longer segment being made of two shorter lengths sewn together. The shorter segment has two leather keepers and galvanized or lacquered steel hardware, and the buckle is equipped with a roller. Shoulder holsters of several different designs were prepared for the Type 94, many by small leather shops, and were popular with aviators and tank crews. A separate, very rare paratrooper holster for the Type 94 is also known. It is made of canvas, has a flap with an oval brass plate and stud closure, and is designed to fit onto the standard paratrooper web belt.

A reproduction of the cowhide holster and strap has recently been imported from China. It is ink-stamped "CHINA" inside of the closure flap, and there are significant dimensional differences in the width of the spare magazine pouch, closure flap hinge, and the strap hanger loops. The strap is 19 mm wide, and its long segment is made of a single piece of leather; fittings are of brass, and the buckle has no roller. A replica canvas holster has also been produced. It can readily be distinguished from the originals by the shape of the body surrounding the mouth of the spare magazine pocket; original holsters have a distinct "C" shaped finger cutout in the fabric at that point, while the replica has only a simple step from "high" at the front to "low" at the rear at this point. Replacement magazines have been produced in the U.S.; they are blued, and are fabricated from much thinner steel than that used in the originals. They function reasonably well, although the feed lips are easily distorted.

The Type 94 cleaning rod may be either nickeled or blued steel, the nickeled variant being the earliest type. It is "L" shaped and 155 mm long, with a 90-degree bend at one end creating a handle that is 25 mm long. The opposite end is flattened and slotted to accept a patch, while the tip is formed into a screwdriver blade. Most nickeled rods, and some blued examples, carry a Kokubunji factory inspection mark. Original Type 94 cleaning rods are rare, because they were stored in the spare magazine pocket in the holster, and were prone to accidental loss during magazine changes. Modern blued reproductions are available, and are easily distinguished from the originals by comparison of the shape of the slotted end.

Ammunition for the Type 94, like that for the Type 14, was packaged in 15-round light brown or tan cardboard boxes. Original boxes are labeled in *kanji* for the Type 94:

九四式拳銃實包
十五發

(On boxes marked for the Type 14, the first characters in the upper line are 十四年式. "Fourteen Year Type.") Type 94 marked cartridge boxes are considerably less common than those marked for the Type 14, and are very desirable collectors items. Reported specimens are dated from 1937-1939 (*Showa* 12-14).

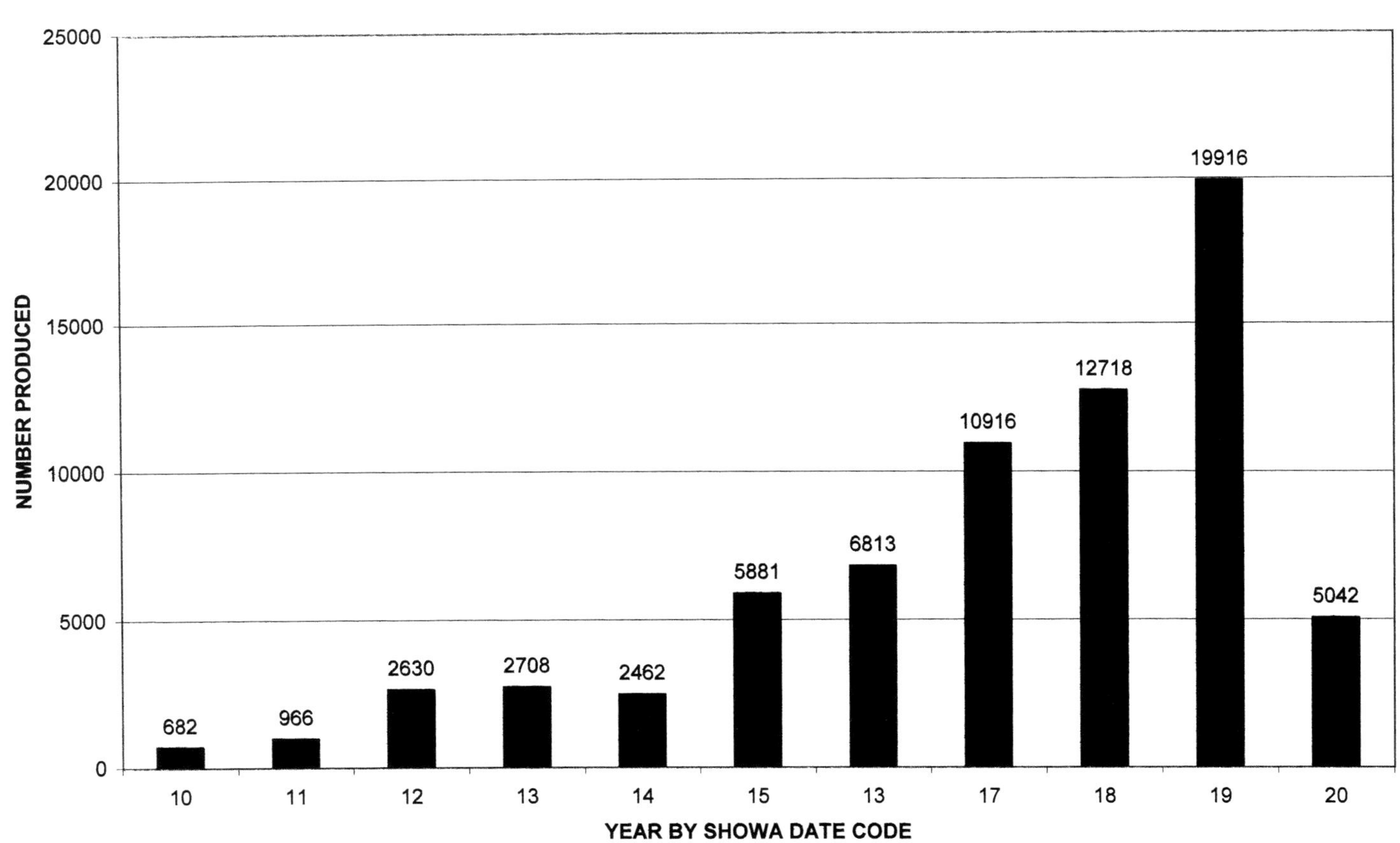

IX

Hamada Pistols

Bunji Hamada was the owner of the Nippon Juki Kabushiki-gaisha (Japan Gun Co., Ltd.), one of several small Japanese civilian manufacturers of sporting arms that were forced into military production as the war in the Pacific began to reach its critical stages. His initial military offering was a 7.65 mm (.32 ACP) pistol of general Browning style, which was adopted in 1941 as the Hamada Type, and was produced at the Japan Gun Co. factory in Tokyo. An estimated 5,000 pistols of this type were produced, but most went to units in China, and were either captured or surrendered to the Communist Chinese at the end of the war. A small number of units armed with the Hamada Type were reassigned to duty in the South Pacific as the war progressed, and known specimens fall into a relatively narrow serial range that was apparently assigned to those units.

In 1942 Japan initiated a program to develop a small pistol in the standard 8 mm caliber as a less expensive replacement for the Type 94. Hamada's entry into the competition was eventually adopted, after numerous modifications mandated by the review board, as the *Ni Shiki*, or Type 2 (for Japanese calendar year 2602). Production of the Type 2 began in Hamada's Notobe factory in 1944, but output never met expectations. In correspondence, Hamada recalled having shipped at least 1,500 Type 2s to the Nagoya Arsenal, although arsenal records confirm receipt of only 500. Only prototypes and production specimens from the 1-50 serial range are known.

7.65 mm Hamada Type pistol, left side view. *Courtesy Harry L. Derby III.*

Identification

The Hamada Type is a 7.65 mm hammerless semiautomatic pistol with its barrel enclosed by a slide. It has fixed sights, is 159 mm (6.26") in length, and weighs 1 lb 8 oz. It is well made, with a deep rust blue finish, and bordered and checkered wooden grip panels retained by a single grip screw on each side. A distinctive grooved takedown latch is located at the rear of the frame immediately above the grip. The slide has seven wide gripping grooves that are rectangular in cross-section, and separated by lands of the same width as the grooves. The left side of the slide has a 10 mm circular recess machined forward of the trigger guard; this recess may or may not contain a stamped inspection mark in the form of a five-petaled cherry blossom (❀). A checkered safety lever is located on the left side of the receiver behind the top of the grip panel, while the magazine latch is located on the butt; a lanyard loop is also provided on the left side of the butt. Markings vary from a full two-line *kanji* type description on the left side of the slide to little more than the *Showa* date and serial number, which are stamped on the right side. The magazine has a capacity of nine cartridges. Several variations are known, differing primarily in external markings. Early *kanji* markings are:

大日本東京 日本銃器株式会社製
浜田式自動拳銃 7.65m/m

They read, from left to right, "Great Japan Tokyo, Japan Gun Company Limited Manufacture, Hamada Type Automatic Handgun 7.65 mm."

The Type 2 Hamada is an 8 mm hammerless semiautomatic pistol with its barrel enclosed by a slide. It has fixed sights, and standard production pistols are 176 mm (6.93") in length, and weigh 1 lb 12 oz. Several prototypes are known that vary signifi-

8 mm Type 2 Hamada pistol serial number 2, left side view. *The Curry Collection, photo by Len Antaris.*

cantly in external dimensions and mechanical characteristics. Prototypes are well finished in a rust blue, while all known production specimens are unfinished, or "in-the-white." Grip panels are made of wood, and on most specimens are checkered, and have two screws with metal escutcheons. Like the Hamada Type, the Type 2 has a distinctive takedown latch located on the rear of the frame immediately above the grip. The slide has six wide gripping grooves that are rectangular in cross-section, and are separated by lands of the same width as the grooves. A grooved safety lever is located on the left side of the frame above and behind the grip panel; the magazine latch is located on the butt. A lanyard loop is located on the left side of the butt. The left side of the slide is marked + 二 式, but in this case the "+" is the symbol of the Notobe factory, not the *kanji* numeral "10." Production pistols also have a pair of large semicircular cut-outs on the upper rear of the slide to reduce weight. Production pistols have a magazine capacity of six cartridges, while prototypes may have magazines holding either six or seven cartridges.

When disassembled, both Hamada models will be found to have a unique method of joining the barrel to the receiver. To dismount the barrel, the muzzle is pivoted 90 degrees to the right, allowing its bottom lug to be removed from a dovetailed recess in the receiver.

Variations

Eight variations of the Hamada Type have been identified, but due to the fact that all known specimens fall into the 2200-2900 serial range, it is quite possible that other variants exist. Detailing the variations in this volume would be counterproductive, as they differ only in external marking and minor external machining patterns, and there are only slightly more than three times as many known specimens as there are recognized variants! Although the earlier variants with full *kanji* slide markings are the most desirable of the 7.65 mm Hamadas, all are rare enough to be of special interest to serious collectors, and individual specimen condition is generally of more importance than variation in determining value. Currently, 27 examples of the Hamada Type are known.

Three different prototype models of the Type 2 were made during its development, and one production prototype without external markings is also known. Eighteen specimens of the production model of the Type 2 are currently known, and although there are some minor differences in markings among these pistols, there are no recognized variants. It is believed that all but the first 50 production pistols were sent to China, where it is possible that a quantity may still remain in storage.

Like other limited production Imperial Japanese handguns, Hamada pistols are difficult to evaluate fairly. The small number of known surviving specimens, together with the number of variants (among 7.65 mm examples), renders any pricing scheme speculative, at best. Reported recent sales of 7.65 mm Hamadas range from $2,500 to $4,500, while those of the 8 mm Type 2 range from $5,000 to $8,000. The increasing number and affluence of potential buyers is expected to generate continuing upward pressure on these prices.

Accessories

A number holster types were apparently made for the Hamada Type, mostly by minor Japanese contractors. They are typically closely fitting, made of cowhide, have one or two black lacquered metal snap fasteners on the closure flap, and may or may not have an attached spare magazine pouch. They are considerably rarer than the pistols themselves.

Type 2 Hamadas have been found housed in standard issue Type 94 holsters; in one case, the holster was hand lettered "Type 2" in *kanji* on the inside of the flap. One very rare variant of the late-war canvas holster associated with the Type 94 is made to slightly larger dimensions, and is believed to have been intended for use with the Type 2, but this cannot be confirmed. No cleaning rods or other tools designed specifically for use with Hamada pistols are known.

X

Inagaki Pistols

The Inagaki Shiki (Inagaki Type) 7.65 mm pistol is the rarest of all handguns officially adopted by the Japanese military. Four specimens are currently known from a total production estimated at 500 pistols. It is quite possible that more unidentified Inagakis are in the U.S., but their lack of recognizable markings may have concealed their identity. Both the Imperial Army and Navy used the Inagaki, and specimens both with and without an encircled naval anchor are known.

A prototype 8 mm Inagaki was also produced for the 1942 program initiated by the Japanese in an effort to develop a less expensive replacement for the Type 94. The prototype was not judged satisfactory, and was never put into production, but at least 9 pistols were apparently fabricated for the trials. Three surviving examples are known.

Identification

The Inagaki Shiki is a straight-blowback 7.65 mm (.32 ACP) semiautomatic pistol with the barrel mostly enclosed by a slide; a 13 mm (½") section of the barrel protrudes from the front. Seven gripping grooves are machined into an enlarged area at the rear of the slide. The grip frame of the Inagaki is farther forward than is common for pistols of its size, giving it excellent balance, but a somewhat unusual appearance. It is 165 mm (6.5") in length, and weighs 1 lb 7 oz. Grip panels are made of wood, are finely diagonally serrated, and each is retained by a single screw. The trigger guard is moveable, and pivots to the left to allow disassembly. The pistol is marked on the left side with its serial number, stamped on the receiver above the front of the trigger guard. The right side of the receiver carries the intertwined letters "I" and "S" ( ) stamped near the rear; naval specimens also have an encircled anchor on the right side of the receiver above the grip panel. The Inagaki has a single-action concealed hammer mechanism. A safety lever is mounted on the right rear of the receiver, with the letter "S" stamped below its pivot to indicate the "safe" position. The magazine catch is located on the butt; the magazine has a capacity of eight cartridges. No lanyard loop is provided. The pistol is finely finished with a deep rust (early) or hot salt (late) blue.

7.65 mm Inagaki Type pistol serial number 391, left side view. *The Curry Collection, photo by Len Antaris.*

8mm Inagaki prototype serial number 101, right side view. *Courtesy Dr. Hiromasa Ikeda, Japan.*

The 8 mm prototype Inagaki is a straight-blowback 8 mm semiautomatic pistol with the barrel mostly enclosed by a slide; like the 7.65 mm model, the muzzle extends approximately ½" beyond the end of the slide. The rear of the slide has a slightly enlarged area with 15 fine gripping grooves. The trigger guard is moveable, and pivots to the left to allow disassembly. The pistol is 180 mm (7.09") in length, and weighs 2 lbs. It has a single-action concealed hammer mechanism. The magazine latch is a push-button located on the left side of the receiver behind the bottom of the trigger guard; the magazine has a capacity of eight cartridges. The safety is a horizontally grooved sliding button located on the left side of the receiver near the rear. Grip panels are diagonally grooved wood, and each is retained by a single screw. The right side of the frame is marked with the serial number and the *kanji* 稲垣式, reading from left to right, *Inagaki Shiki*. Exterior finish is relatively rough, with hot salt blueing.

Variations

Two variants of the 7.65 mm Inagaki are known, the Army version (without property markings) and the Navy version, with encircled anchor. The rarity of the Inagaki makes the variant insignificant in determining a specimen's value. No variation is known among specimens of the 8 mm prototype Inagaki.

Because of the extremely small number of surviving specimens (three 7.65 mm production pistols and three 8 mm prototypes are known), attempting to establish values for these pistols would be meaningless. For appraisal purposes, any number between $10,000 and $15,000 would be reasonable, but actual value can only be established by offering individual specimens at auction before an audience of well informed collectors.

Accessories

Serial no. 164 is accompanied by a well made cowhide holster of Japanese design. It has a horizontally mounted spare magazine pouch with snap closure. No other holsters or accessories for the Inagaki are known.

XI

North China Type 19

The North China Type 19 (derived from 1944, *Showa* 19, the year of its adoption) is a rare and interesting example of Japan's effort to enlist Chinese industry in its war effort as the weight of the combined Allied assault began to bear heavily on its industrial capabilities. The Type 19 is clearly an adaptation of the Type 14, with modifications that were intended primarily to simplify manufacture, although there are also some operational improvements included in the design. The identity of the designer is unknown.

The Type 19 was produced at two different factories, resulting in the two principal variants. Output was not great; probably no more than a total of 200 pistols were produced, and only 20 examples from both variants are known. Because of their rarity the pistols are not widely recognized by collectors, and can easily be mistaken for Type 14s by the casual observer. With proper identification they command very respectable prices.

Identification

The Type 19 is an 8 mm semiautomatic pistol with a 119 mm (4.7") exposed barrel, fixed sights, a knurled cocking knob of grooved cylindrical shape mounted on the rear of the bolt, and a trigger guard that is integral with the receiver. It has a 65 degree grip angle, horizontally grooved wooden grip panels, and an 8-round magazine with a grooved aluminum alloy base. It is 232 mm (9.13") to 235 mm (9.25") in length, and weighs 2 lbs 5 oz. to 2 lb 7 oz (differences in size and weight relate to the two manufacturing variants). It has a safety lever mounted on the left side of the receiver behind the top of the grip panel, and a takedown lever mounted on the right side of the receiver forward of the trigger guard.

Markings

The left side of the receiver carries the stamped *kanji* 北支一九式, reading "North China Nineteen Type," and a serial number. The type marking is larger on the second variation than on the first. Some internal parts are marked with an assembly number that is apparently unrelated to the serial number. First variation specimens carry concentric circle markings associated with Tientsin Arsenal (◎); second variation pistols carry the encircled *kanji NI* (㊁), indicating a second class weapon, and probably reflecting their

North China Type 19 first variation serial number 18, left side view. *The Curry Collection, photo by Len Antaris.*

North China Type 19 second variation serial number 063, left side view. *The Curry Collection, photo by Len Antaris.*

noticeably lower quality than the first variation. Second variation pistols generally carry an inspection mark immediately to the right of the type *kanji*. Serial no. 10 carries a single *kanji* safety mark, while serial no. 35 has both "safe" and "fire" safety *kanji*; other known specimens lack safety markings.

Variations

The two manufacturing variants of the Type 19 are easily distinguished by their serial numbers and grip panel styles. Variation 1 has serial numbers with one or two digits, and has grip panels with 19 deeply machined horizontal grooves. Thirteen examples of this variant are known, from the serial range 4-55. Variation 2 has three-digit serial numbers beginning with one or more zeros, and has grip panels that are lightly hand-cut with varying numbers of horizontal grooves and a border. There are also slight differences in the contours of the trigger guard and front sight, and in the take-down lever and its pivot. Machining and finish quality on Variation 2 pistols is inferior to Variation 1. Seven Variation 2 examples are known, from the serial range 004-093.

Values of North China Type 19 pistols are highly variable, simply because they are not well known, and their rarity is often not recognized. Recently reported sales have ranged from $2,500 to $8,000.

Accessories

The Type 19 was issued with a matching second magazine and a leather holster with shoulder strap. Authenticated holsters are of typical Chinese construction under Japanese control, with metal snap closures. The Type 19 will also fit comfortably in the standard Type 14 holster. No other tools or accessories specifically designed for this pistol are known.

XII

Sugiura Pistols

The Sugiura is not truly a Japanese made pistol, although it was developed by the Japanese, and was initially produced under Japanese direction in China. The design is most probably Japanese, although it shows strong influence from the Model 1903 Browning, and evidently was developed by a member of the ancient Japanese family whose name is attached to the pistol. It was produced in two different models, one in 7.65 mm (.32 ACP) and the other in 6.35 mm (.25 ACP). Production of both models was continued by the Chinese without the Japanese markings after the war, creating a total of four primary variants. All are rare, but the Sugiura probably suffers more than other Japanese military handguns from lack of familiarity, and thus reduced collector interest. It deserves more attention.

Identification

Both the 6.35 mm and 7.65 mm Sugiuras are straight-blowback semiautomatic pistols with their barrels fully enclosed by a slide. They have fixed sights and a single-action concealed hammer mechanism. Both resemble the Model 1903 7.65 mm Colt/Browning in general configuration, the 6.35 mm being notably smaller (although not as small as the 6.35 mm Browning) and the 7.65 mm slightly larger. Both have detachable magazines with a capacity of eight cartridges; the magazine catch is located on the rear of the butt. Both have safety levers located on the left side. Grip panels are made of wood, and are bordered and patterned in a manner that is more accurately described as crosshatched, rather than checkered. The 6.35 mm model is 140 mm (5.51") in length and weighs 1 lb 1 oz, while the 7.65 mm model is 180 mm (7.09") in length and weighs 2 lbs.

7.65 mm Sugiura serial number 2835 (upper) and 6.35 mm Sugiura serial number 183, right side views. *Ron L. Payne Collection, photo by Terrill Hoffman.*

Markings

The Japanese variants of both models are marked on the right side of the receiver in *kanji* 杉浦式, *Sugiura Shiki* ("Sugiura Type") and the serial number, which is also stamped on the right side of the slide. The Chinese variants are generally marked ☆北工, roughly translated "North China Industry."

Variations

As noted above, both a Japanese and a Chinese variant of each model was produced. There are six known specimens of the Japanese 6.35 mm model, serial nos. 103, 113, 173, 183, 224, and 422. Twenty-seven specimens of the Japanese 7.65 mm model are known, in the serial range 1012-3323. Estimated production of the Japanese variants is 430 6.35 mm pistols and 2,330 7.65 mm pistols.

There are three known specimens of the Chinese 6.35 mm model, serial nos. 435, 445, and 475. Of the Chinese 7.65 mm model 13 specimens are known, in the serial range 3,343-5,839. Estimated total production of the Chinese variants is 50 6.35 mm pistols and 2,550 7.65 mm pistols.

Valuation of the Sugiura is challenging, because its rarity is offset by its lack of familiarity among collectors. It is among the least known of Imperial Japanese handguns, and its external appearance can easily lead to confusion of its identity as "another cheap Browning clone." No recent sales have been reported, so there is no solid foundation upon which to base an appraisal. In general, the range of $5,000 to $10,000 is probably reasonable on the basis of rarity, with 6.35 mm specimens closer to the upper end of this range, and 7.65 mm specimens closer to the lower end. Chinese variants are clearly rarer than those with Japanese markings, but the latter are more likely to be in fine condition, and are generally of greater interest to the collector of Japanese arms.

Accessories

Two types of holsters were made for the Japanese 7.65 mm model. One was apparently fabricated by the same contractor that made the majority of the soft-shell "Baby" Nambu holsters; it is made of pigskin, with straps and brass furniture of the same type used on the "Baby" holster, and looks very much like a "Baby" holster with a wider butt and a shorter, squared-off bottom. The second type is similar to the holsters usually encountered with Hamada Type 7.65 mm pistols, and is made of cowhide with metal snap closures on the flap, and an external spare magazine pouch also with a snap closure flap. The only known holsters for the 6.35 mm model resemble scaled down versions of the cowhide holster for the 7.65 mm model.

No information on holsters for the Chinese variants of the Sugiura is currently available. There are no known cleaning rods or other tools that were specifically designed for Sugiura pistols.

XIII

Special Naval Pistols

In the closing months of World War II, the Imperial Navy developed two types of pistols that were intended to replace conventional rifles and submachineguns for guards serving on naval bases. These were originally thought to be signal pistols, but research by Japanese historians has uncovered documentation confirming their actual purpose. Both accept standard 12-gauge shotgun cartridges, and both are equipped with sights. Both types were produced by the Yokosuka Naval Arsenal; they are very crudely executed, and are finished with black lacquer. They carry both a serial number and a separate assembly number, an oddly complex arrangement for such arms. Although these are technically short-barreled shotguns, they have been classified by the Bureau of Alcohol, Tobacco, Firearms, and Explosives as "Curios and Relics," and are thus legal to own. Because of their questionable construction quality, attempting to fire these weapons is strongly discouraged.

The double-barrel Type 4 pistol is 264 mm (10.39") in length, with 165 mm (6.5") barrels, a cast grip frame, and molded plastic grip panels. It weighs 2 lbs 12 oz, and has dual internal strikers that are cocked by the unbreeching action of the barrel. A barrel latch is located on the top of the breech, and the pistol is equipped with a barrel selector and a safety lever. Fourteen examples are known, with a serial number range of 14-328.

The single-barrel pistol (labeled the "Type 5" on the speculative assumption that it was adopted later than the Type 4, although no official Japanese model designation is known) is 267 mm (10.5") in length with a 210 mm (8¼") barrel and a grip frame, and most parts fabricated from sheet metal stampings. It has an external hammer that must be manually cocked; an unbreeching lever is located next to the hammer. Only two examples are known, serial nos. 50 and 121.

Valuation of these arms is an exercise in speculation, as their undeniable rarity is more than offset by the crudeness of their design and execution, and there is little in the way of reported sales on which to base an appraisal. One owner of a pair of "Type 5" pistols has offered them repeatedly at gun shows for a price of $2,500 apiece without drawing much interest, but it is also likely that few potential customers saw them as anything more than a "crude zip-gun." Current values can reasonably be assumed to be between $1,000 and $2,000, depending upon individual characteristics and condition, but the potential buyer remains at the mercy of the seller because of rarity.

12 gauge Special Naval Pistol Type 4, left side view. *Courtesy Harry L. Derby.*

12 gauge Special Naval Pistol "Type 5" (actual Japanese model designation not known), right side view. *Courtesy Harry L. Derby III.*

XIV

Signal Pistols

Signal pistols were developed by Japan beginning in 1921, primarily for use from aircraft, although other uses were adopted over time. In rather typical fashion, the Imperial Army and Navy proceeded in different directions. The Army adopted a single-barrel design chambered for a 35 mm cartridge, and with only minor changes retained this design through the end of World War II. The Navy adopted a completely different 28 mm cartridge, and progressed through four different pistol designs chambered for it, most equipped with multiple barrels. All Japanese signal pistols are scarce in comparison to conventional military handguns—they were made in smaller numbers, they were considered somewhat less desirable as souvenirs by American GIs, and a significant proportion of them were lost in combat together with the planes and ships that carried them.

The Type 10

The Type 10 is a single-barreled 35 mm pistol adopted by the Imperial Army in 1921 (*Taisho* 10). It uses the same double-action-only lockwork design as the Type 26 revolver, and resembles it superficially, except for the size of the barrel and absence of a cylinder. Its barrel latch is a grooved push-down button, rather than the pull-up yoke used on the Type 26. It is 211 mm (8.31") in length and weighs 2 lbs 10 oz. Grip panels are made of horizontally grooved beech, and are retained by two screws passing all the way through both panels. Approximately 8,300 Type 10 pistols were produced by the Tokyo and Kokura Arsenals through the end of World War II.

35 mm Type 10 signal pistol (early production), left side view. *Courtesy Harry L. Derby III.*

Markings on the Type 10 consist of the Tokyo/Kokura arsenal symbol, the *kanji* 十年式 ("Ten Year Type") markings, and the serial number. Early Type 10s are marked on both the right and left sides, while later pistols show only left side markings. One or more inspection marks are usually stamped on the lower front of the grip frame.

Early Type 10 production at the Tokyo Arsenal was relatively low; only about 1400 pistols were made in the first 13 years of production. By early 1935 (serial no. 1430), production had been moved to the second factory of Kokura Arsenal, where some 5,600 Type 10s were produced over the next nine years. By November 1944 (approximately serial no 7000) production had again been moved to the Kasuga factory of Kokura Arsenal, where the final 1,300 pistols were assembled.

The only significant recognized variant of the Type 10 is a short-lived modification that incorporates a safety lever on the left side. This addition was evidently recognized rather quickly as an unnecessary and expensive addition and was dropped; only four examples are known, from the 313-453 serial range. There is also a series of minor "evolutionary variations" in the Type 10 involving the shape of the trigger guard, thickness and length of grip panels, and type and quality of external machining and finishing. While it is fairly simple to distinguish more finely made "early" guns from the more crudely executed "late" ones, no effort has been made to classify these into defined variants.

A series of holster variants were produced for the Type 10. Early holsters are made of cowhide leather, while later models utilized canvas lined oilcloth, rubberized canvas of the same type used in late-war Type 14 holsters, and plain canvas with leather fittings. A folding screwdriver was provided, and fits into a small pocket stitched to the front of the holster; specimens are scarce. Both standard and improvised lanyards were used with the Type 10.

35 mm Signal Cartridges

Japanese 35 mm cartridges are 120 mm in length, and may either be formed from brass, or may utilize a cardboard body with a brass base. *Kanji* stamped on the base indicate the projectile contents. The cartridges are of two basic types. "Dragon" (龍) cartridges contain suspended smoke signals with parachutes of the same color as the smoke, and were designed for daylight use. "Star" (星) cartridges contain single or multiple burning colored "stars," and may be used during daylight, although they are most visible during darkness. The rims of 35 mm star cartridges are notched in a pattern to allow determination of the color in the dark. (No notches = yellow, 1/3 circumference = white, ½ circumference = red, 2/3 circumference = blue [not confirmed by direct examination], and full circumference = green.) In addition to the "dragon" and "star" characters, headstamps may contain the *kanji* numerals 1, 2, or 3 (一, 二, or 三, respectively), the *kanji* for the colors white, yellow, red, green, blue, or black (白, 黄, 赤, 緑, 青, and 黒, respectively), and the *kanji* 吊 ("suspended") for parachute flares.

First Kayaba 28 mm Double-Barrel

The initial signal pistol design adopted by the Imperial Navy in 1927 was a 28 mm double-barrel model with dual exposed hammers. These pistols are very well made, but they were apparently not well liked, because the grip design did not dissipate recoil well, and they were thus unpleasant to shoot. In profile, these pistols resemble shortened conventional double-barrel shotguns with rounded grips, dual triggers, long, curved trigger guards, and a conventional sliding button safety at the upper end of the grip, but they are much more massive across the breech area. They are 197 mm (7.76") in length, with 103 mm (4.06") barrels, and weigh 2 lbs 8 oz. A hooked unbreeching lever is located under the barrels.

Two significant variants exist: the standard model produced by Kayaba, and a subcontracted version produced by Tokyo Gas Electric Co. They can be readily distinguished by differences in the shape of the trigger guard and by the Kayaba () or TGE () logo stamped on the upper grip frame. The TGE variant is considerably rarer than the standard production Kayaba pistol; only two TGE specimens are known, the highest serial number being 31. Kayaba produced pistols used a separate serial series, with known specimens spanning the 12-407 serial range.

Leather holsters were provided for the Kayaba pistols, apparently of a somewhat different pattern than those used with later Type 90 Two-barrel pistols. Because both models will fit the early holsters, it has not been possible to state with certainty which pistol these early holsters were intended to house.

Kayaba Type 90

General dissatisfaction with the original Kayaba Double-Barrel design led to the development of revised 28 mm designs adopted by the Imperial Navy in 1930 (Japanese calendar year 2590) and 1932, and designated the Type 90. (The double-barrel model was given the same designation as the triple-barrel, even though it was adopted two years later.) The Type 90 was produced in both a two-barrel and a three-barrel model; both utilize a more vertical grip frame, and an internal buffering mechanism designed to reduce felt recoil. Type 90 pistols are 185 mm (7.28") in length with 103 mm (4.06") barrels; the two-barrel model weighs 2 lbs 12 oz, while the three-barrel model weighs 3 lbs 11 oz. Two-barrel pistols utilize a straight-pull cocking lever mounted on the rear of the breech, while the three-barrel model has a rotary cocking lever mounted in the same position. Both models employ a barrel selector lever mounted at the upper rear of the grip frame, and a safety lever mounted on the left side behind the top of the grip panel. The bores of both models are 28 mm in diameter, but are tapered to 26.5 mm at the muzzle.

Both two- and three-barrel models went through a series of design modifications that were intended to improve operation and facilitate construction. These modifications include the unbreeching lever design, grip frame contour and material, grip panel material and shape, exterior finish, markings, and a number of other

Kayaba 28 mm double-barrel signal pistol serial number 71, right side view. *Robert E. Hogan collection, photo by Scott T. Hogan.*

Kayaba Type 90 Two-barrel signal pistol, first variation. *The Curry Collection, photo by Len Antaris.*

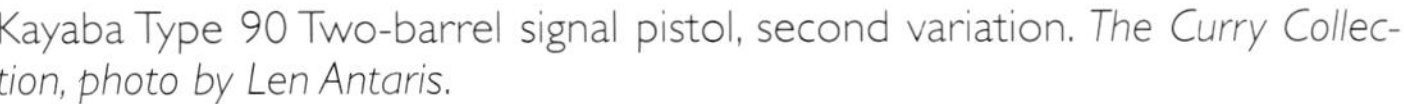

Kayaba Type 90 Two-barrel signal pistol, second variation. *The Curry Collection, photo by Len Antaris.*

Kayaba Type 90 Two-barrel signal pistol, third variation. *The Curry Collection, photo by Len Antaris.*

minor changes. These changes have been categorized into three principle variants on the basis of the unbreeching lever style, with most other modifications paralleling the lever style changes, but overlapping and secondary modifications create a broad array of sub-variants that have not been thoroughly catalogued. Because of frequent and large gaps in the serial numbers between observed specimens precise definition of the changes between variants is not possible, and the serial ranges assigned to each should be considered only as crude estimates.

Variation	Unbreeching Lever Shape	Exterior Finish	Grip Frame Material	Grip Panel Material	Approximate Serial Ranges
1	Vertical contoured	Rust blued	Steel	Wood or plastic	2B: 1-3,900 3B: 1-1,400
2	Vertical straight	Black lacquer	Steel	Plastic	2B: 3,900-7,050 3B: 1,400-4,800
3	Horizontal crescent	Hot salt blue/ black lacquer	Cast alloy	Plastic	2B: 7,050-10,500 3B: 4,800-5,100

Kayaba Type 90 Three-barrel signal pistol, second variation. External differences among the Three-barrel variations are the same as those among Two-barrel variants. *Courtesy Harry L. Derby III.*

Only about half as many Type 90 Three-Barrel pistols were produced as its two-barrel contemporary. This, coupled with its status as the only three-barrel signal pistol manufactured by any nation, gives it a noteworthy position as a collectors' item.

A very rare variant of the three-barrel model was evidently produced, probably as a precursor to the standard production run. It carries the KFC logo of the Kawaguchiya Firearms Company stamped on the left side of the frame. Only one example, serial no. 5, is known. No similar two-barrel variant is known, and it is doubtful that it was produced, as Type 90 three-barrel model production was well under way by the time the two-barrel model was approved.

Holsters for Type 90 pistols are made of cowhide leather with a variety of external surface treatments; all are rare. Fittings are made of brass, nickel plated brass, or galvanized steel. Shoulder straps were originally made in three segments, but one or more of these is often cut or missing from surviving examples.

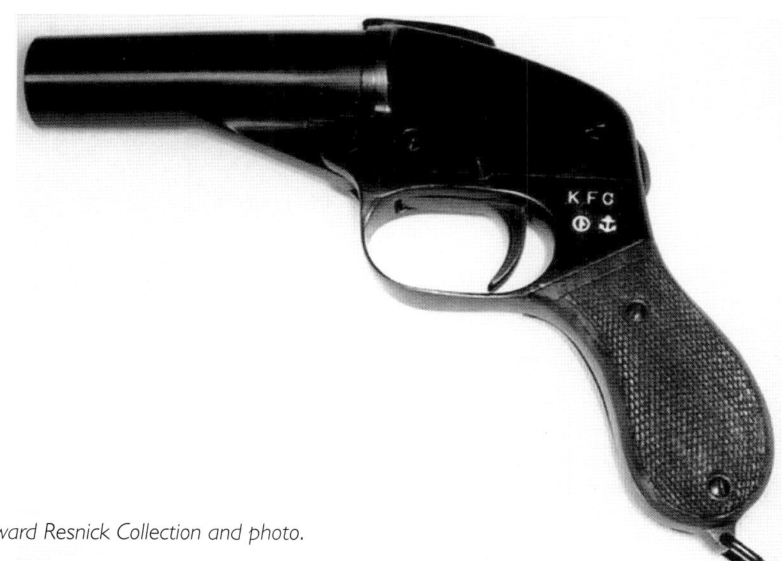

Type 97 signal pistol serial number 1710, left side view. *Howard Resnick Collection and photo.*

Type 97

The Type 97 28 mm signal pistol was developed by the Kawaguchiya Firearms Co., and was adopted by the Imperial Navy in 1937 (Japanese calendar year 2597). It is the only Japanese single-barreled 28 mm design, and is prized by collectors because of its elegantly simple lines and its scarcity. The Type 97 is 212 mm (8.35") in length with a 103 mm (4.06") barrel, and weighs 1 lb 11 oz. It is of all-steel construction except for the finely checkered wood grip panels. It incorporates an internal cocking mechanism that is activated by movement of the barrel during unbreeching. An estimated 3,250 Type 97s were produced; they can be subdivided into five variations based on left side exterior frame markings.

Variation	Markings	Known Serial Range
1	KFC	126-145*
2	KFC ㋣ ⚓ (note small size relative to KFC logo)	1710-2311*
3	KFC ㋣ ⚓	2525-3027
4	屋口川 ㋣ ⚓	3119-3191
5	㋣ ⚓	3200

*The large serial gap between these variants makes estimation of total production for each impossible, but it is thought that the naval inspection marks were probably added relatively early.

The Type 97 was provided with a very well made cowhide leather holster with shoulder strap. These holsters were designed to be worn on the left side with the pistol butt facing forward, so that they did not interfere with a conventional sidearm carried on the right side.

28 mm Signal Cartridges

Japanese 28 mm signal cartridges are 90-94 mm in length, and consist of a cardboard body and a metal base. Early cartridge bases are brass, while those on late-production cartridges are made of lacquered steel. Like 35 mm cartridges, the 28 mm rounds were produced in two basic types, "dragons" and "stars." "Dragon" cartridges have case mouth plugs marked with the character 龍, while "star' cartridges have unmarked plugs. The cartridge body color indicates the color of the signal it contains (white, yellow, red, blue, green, or black), while a glued-on paper label indicates the manufacturer, production year and month, and in most cases a "category" (Lot) identified by an English letter. The character 艦 ("warship") in the manufacturer identification column of most, but not all, cartridges refers to the Naval Ordnance Board. Characters used in label dates include several archaic *kanji* that are used in texts as substitutes for conventional numerals; these include 壱 and 壹 (one); 弐 and 貳 (two); 参 (three); and 拾 (ten). The use of these "extra" characters for numbers in texts was an ancient development intended to prevent accounting fraud, in which strokes were added to the *kanji* numbers 1 and 2 to change them to 3 or 10. Examples of 28 mm signal cartridge labels are as follows:

昭和拾六年七月製
種目 **L**
日火∩艦∪

Yellow dragon, Lot L,
made in *Showa* 16.7made in *Showa* 17.2

昭和拾七年弐月製
種目 **N**
日火∩艦∪

Yellow dragon, Lot N,
made in *Showa* 19.1

昭和拾九年壹月製
日火∩艦∪

Black dragon, no Lot,

Both Japanese signal pistols and their cartridges and accessories are of interest to specialized collectors. Because this group is relatively small sales tend to be slow, and prices often do not reflect the items' true rarity. Fine specimens deserve careful marketing. Type 10 pistols currently bring from $350 to $650, depending on condition and production period, with the earliest guns generally commanding the highest prices. There are too few reports of recent sales of Kayaba 28 mm Double-Barrel pistols to form a meaningful basis for evaluation, but values in the $1,000 to $2,500 range are reasonable, based on rarity and interest. Kayaba Type 90 Two-Barrel pistols are the most common Imperial Japanese Navy design, and typically sell at prices ranging from $250 to $550, depending on variant and condition. Type 90 Three-Barrel pistols in very good condition typically bring prices ranging from $750 to $1,200, again depending on variant and individual pistol characteristics; the fact that these were the only three-barrel signal pistols produced by any nation adds to their overall appeal. The KFC Type 97 Signal Pistol benefits from rarity, number of variants, and the overall elegance of its design, but reports of recent sales are nearly nonexistent as a basis for evaluation. The value of a specimen in very good condition should fall into the $1,500 to $2,500 range.

Japanese 35 mm signal cartridges are rare; loaded cartridges may bring prices of $250 to $450, and even empty cases will generally bring $200 or more. The 28 mm cartridges are encountered somewhat more frequently, but are by no means common, and typically sell for $125 to $200. Signal pistol holsters vary widely in price depending on model, variant, and condition, and may range in value from about $100 to more than $750; an original strap generally adds $100 to $150 to the value of the holster.

Subject Index